Guidance notes and flow charts for the

Term Service Short Contract

This contract should be used for the appointment of a supplier for a period of time to manage and provide a service

The NEC3 Term Service Short Contract is an alternative to the NEC3 Term Service Contract and is for use with contracts which do not require sophisticated management techniques, comprise straightforward work and impose only low risks on both the Employer and the Contractor

An NEC document

September 2008

OGC endorsement of NEC3

OGC advises public sector procurers that the form of contract used has to be selected according to the objectives of the project, aiming to satisfy the *Achieving Excellence in Construction* (AEC) principles.

This edition of the NEC (NEC3) complies fully with the AEC principles. OGC recommends the use of NEC3 by public sector construction procurers on their construction projects.

Office of Government Commerce

NEC is a division of Thomas Telford Ltd, which is a wholly owned subsidiary of the Institution of Civil Engineers (ICE), the owner and developer of the NEC.

The NEC is a family of standard contracts, each of which has these characteristics:

- Its use stimulates good management of the relationship between the two parties to the contract and, hence, of the work included in the contract.
- It can be used in a wide variety of commercial situations, for a wide variety of types of work and in any location.
- It is a clear and simple document – using language and a structure which are straightforward and easily understood.

These guidance notes and flow charts are for the Term Service Short Contract which is both part of the NEC family and are consistent with all other NEC3 documents.

ISBN (complete box set) 978-07277-3382-5
ISBN (this document) 978-07277-3619-2
ISBN (Term Service Short Contract) 978-07277-3618-5

First edition 2008
Reprinted 2009

Cover photo, Golden Jubilee Bridge, courtesy of City of Westminster

9 8 7 6 5 4 3 2

British Library Cataloguing in Publication Data for this publication is available from the British Library.

Typeset by Academic + Technical, Bristol

Printed and bound in Great Britain by Bell & Bain Limited, Glasgow, UK

CONTENTS

ACKNOWLEDGEMENTS

The first edition of the NEC Term Service Short Contract was produced by the Institution of Civil Engineers through its NEC Panel. It was mainly drafted by Bill Weddell based on work by Andrew Baird.

The Flow Charts were produced by Ross Hayes.

The original NEC was designed and drafted by Dr Martin Barnes then of Coopers and Lybrand with the assistance of Professor J. G. Perry then of The University of Birmingham, T. W. Weddell then of Travers Morgan Management, T. H. Nicholson, Consultant to the Institution of Civil Engineers, A. Norman then of the University of Manchester Institute of Science and Technology and P. A. Baird, then Corporate Contracts Consultant, Eskom, South Africa.

The members of the NEC Panel are:

N. C. Shaw, FCIPS, CEng, MIMechE (Chairman)
P. A. Baird, BSc, CEng, FICE, M(SA)ICE, MAPM
A. J. M. Blackler, BA, LLB(Cantab), MCIArb
M. Codling, BSc, ICIOB, MAPM
L. T. Eames, BSc, FRICS, FCIOB
M. Garratt, BSc(Hons), MRICS, FCIArb
J. J. Lofty, MRICS

NEC Consultant:

R. A. Gerrard, BSc(Hons), FRICS, FCIArb, FInstCES

Secretariat:

J. M. Hawkins, BA(Hons), MSc
S. Hernandez, BSc, MSc

INTRODUCTION

| The notes in boxes like this one | printed within the NEC Term Service Short Contract (TSSC), explain how to complete TSSC when it is used for a simple, low risk contract. These boxed notes are reproduced in these guidance notes, which also explain the background to the TSSC and give guidance for its use as a main contract. The flow charts show the procedural logic on which the TSSC is based and are published in this volume for reference.

In these guidance notes, as in the contract itself, terms which are defined in the TSSC have capital initials and those which are identified in the Contract Data are in italics. The guidance notes and the flow charts are not part of the TSSC and have no legal function.

WHEN TO USE THE TSSC

Within the NEC family, the TSSC is the alternative to the Term Service Contract (TSC) and is for use with contracts which

- do not require sophisticated management techniques,
- comprise straightforward work and
- impose only low risks on both the *Employer* and the *Contractor*.

Users choosing between the TSSC and the TSC should base their choice purely on the level of complexity of the work required and the level of risk to each of the Parties.

THE TSSC PACKAGE

The TSSC package includes the conditions of contract and forms which, when filled in (except for the Task Order form), make up a complete contract. The forms are on pages 1 to 9 of the package and are provided for

- the title page and the Contract Forms comprising
- Contract Data
- The *Contractor*'s Offer,
- The *Employer*'s Acceptance,
- Price List,
- Service Information and
- Task Order.

Stage A: How an *Employer* invites tenders for a job

Examples using a fictitious small building job are appended to these notes to illustrate how the title page and Contract Forms should be filled in at each of the following three stages leading to a contract.

The *Employer* uses the package to invite tenders for proposed services by providing the following information on the forms and sending the package to tenderers with the invitation to tender.

- **The title page (page 1) – see example A1**
- **Contract Data (pages 2 & 3) – see example A2**
- **The *Contractor*'s Offer and the *Employer*'s Acceptance (page 4) – leave blank**
- **Price List (page 5) – see notes on subclause 50.2**

> The Price List is in two parts. Part 1 is for work described in the Service Information not requiring the *Employer* to issue a Task Order. Part 2 is for work to be carried out within a stated period of time on a Task by Task basis and instructed by Task Order. The Service may comprise work under Part 1 only or Part 2 only or a mix of both.
>
> Entries in the first four columns of Part 1 of the Price List are made either by the *Employer* or the tenderer. Entries in the first four columns of Part 2 of the Price List would normally be made by the *Employer* as the Party most likely to know the kind of work which will be instructed by the issue of Task Orders. The tenderer then enters a rate for each item and multiplies it by the Expected quantity to produce the Price to be entered in the final column.
>
> If the *Contractor* is to be paid an amount for the item which is not adjusted if the quantity of work in the item changes, the tenderer enters the amount in the Price column only, the Unit, Expected quantity and Rate columns being left blank.
>
> If the *Contractor* is to be paid an amount for the item of work which is the rate for the work multiplied by the quantity completed, the tenderer enters a rate for each item and multiplies it by the Expected quantity to produce the Price, to be entered in the final column.
>
> If the *Contractor* is to be paid a Price for an item proportional to the length of time for which a service is provided, a unit of time is stated in the Unit column and the expected length of time (as a quantity of the stated units of time) is stated in the Expected quantity column.

- **Service Information (pages 6–8) (see notes on subclauses 11.2(5) and 60.1(1))**

> The Service Information should be a complete and precise statement of the *Employer*'s requirements. If it is incomplete or imprecise there is a risk that the *Contractor* will interpret it differently from the *Employer*'s intention. The Service Information should state clearly the part of the *service* which is to be carried out by the *Contractor* and which does not require the *Employer* to issue a Task Order. This part of the *service* is priced in Part 1 of the Price List. Information provided by the *Contractor* should be listed in the Service Information only if the *Employer* is satisfied that it is required, is part of a complete statement of the *Employer*'s requirements and is consistent with the other parts of the Service Information.

1 Description of the *service*

> Give a detailed description of what the *Contractor* is required to do. This may include drawings.

2 Specifications

> List the specifications that apply to this contract.

It is important that these are thoroughly prepared and comprehensive because the TSSC definition of a Defect (subclause 11.2(1)) is based entirely on the Service Information. Include in the specifications details of

- quality standards for design (if any) and workmanship,
- any tests and testing procedures required and
- any specific equipment and methods of construction to be used.

3 Constraints on how the *Contractor* Provides the Service

> State any constraints on the sequence and timing of work and on the methods and conduct of work including the requirements for any work by the *Employer*.

Refer to any specific constraints relating to the country where the *service* is to be provided. These may include provisions such as a labour intensive approach using appropriate technology, and maximising local employment.

The *Contractor* should be allowed to subcontract work without any limit (subclause 21.1). However, the *Employer* may wish to limit the extent of subcontracting if, for example, the *Contractor* is being selected for a particular expertise. The *Employer* may also wish to provide lists of subcontractors and suppliers who would be acceptable for specific categories of work or supplies. Any such constraints should be stated here.

If the *Contractor*'s work needs to be co-ordinated with other activities or contracts, define the parts of the *service* affected and state the dates by which each is to be completed.

If the *Contractor*'s work is to be affected by work done by the *Employer*, the nature of the *Employer*'s work, including the timing should be stated.

4 Requirements for the plan

> State whether a plan is required and, if it is, state what form it is to be in, what information is to be shown on it, when it is to be submitted and when it is to be updated.

The plan is an important document for administering the contract. It informs the *Employer* of the *Contractor*'s detailed intentions of how and at what times he is to Provide the Service. It enables the *Employer* to monitor the *Contractor*'s performance and to assess the effects of compensation events.

5 Services and other things provided by the *Employer*

> Describe what the *Employer* will provide, such as services (including water and electricity) and 'free issue' plant, materials and equipment.

The descriptions should include the capacities available and the location of connection points.

Any equipment, information or other things which the *Employer* wishes to take over from the *Contractor* at, or soon after the end of the service period, should be listed (subclause 70.2).

6 Property affected by the *service*

> Give information about any property affected by the *service* and any other information which is likely to affect the *Contractor*'s work.

- **Invitation to tender**

The *Employer*'s invitation to tender should include a list of suggested adjudicators from which the tenderers are asked to choose one (see notes on subclause 93.2).

The invitation to tender may also include other matters, for example

- any constraints on how the Price List should be used for the submission of tenders,
- if the *Employer* requires tenderers to give names and details of supervisory staff, equipment and methods to be used in Providing the Service, the information should be requested in the invitation to tender (normally, it should be stated that any such details should not form part of the contract and are provided for information only),
- in some circumstances the *Employer* may also wish to draw the attention of tenderers to local employment legislation and health and safety legislation and may also emphasise the importance of gender equality (equal opportunities, equal pay for work of equal value), minimum age of employment and protection of wages (to ensure wages are paid on time and in cash).

Stage B: How a tenderer makes an offer

A tenderer uses the package to make an offer by providing information on the following forms.

- Price List (page 5) – see notes under Stage A and on subclause 50.2.
- The *Contractor*'s Offer (page 4) – see example B1

> Enter the total of the Prices from the Price List.

The tenderer's covering letter should also include

- the tenderer's choice of adjudicator from the list suggested by the *Employer* or, if none is acceptable, the tenderer's own suggestions,
- any extra Service Information proposed by the tenderer and

- any additional information asked for by the *Employer* in the invitation to tender, such as
  - names and particulars of tenderer's supervisory staff or workforce proposed and
  - proposals for equipment or methods to be used.

The letter should also make it clear if any part of the *Contractor*'s Offer does not comply with the Contract Data or the Service Information provided by the *Employer*.

Stage C: How a contract is made

The package becomes the complete contract document when the *Employer* makes the following additional entries and sends a copy to the *Contractor* who has made the chosen offer.

- The *Employer*'s Acceptance of the offer (page 4) – see example C1.
- The title page (page 1) – *Contractor*'s name added – see example C2.
- The Contract Forms including the Contract Data (page 3) – *Adjudicator*'s name added – see example C3.

Under the law of England and Wales, the contract between the *Employer* and the *Contractor* is then made. There may be other requirements in other jurisdictions.

The TSSC uses a simple offer (The *Contractor*'s Offer, page 4) and acceptance (The *Employer*'s Acceptance, page 4) to create a contract. It is emphasised that this is the most efficient and clear way of creating a simple contract and users should aim to achieve this. However, if

- the tenderer's covering letter requires changes to the documents (other than to incorporate the addition of the accepted *Adjudicator*) or
- the *Employer* has issued supplements to the invitation to tender amending the documents,

these need to be recorded with the *Contractor*'s Offer or the *Employer*'s Acceptance.

The *Employer* adding into the *Employer*'s Acceptance before this is achieved either by

- the tenderer adding after the offered total of the Prices

  'This offer includes our covering letter

  Reference . . . . Dated . . . . ' or

- the signature

  'The Offer includes the information provided in . . . . '.

(This is either the tenderer's covering letter if not already mentioned in the *Contractor*'s Offer or a document or summary agreed by the two parties after the tender was received.)

NOTES ON THE CLAUSES

1 General

Actions **10**

10.1   This clause obliges the *Employer* and the *Contractor* to do everything which the contract states each of them does. It is the only clause which uses the future tense. For simplicity, everything else is in the present tense.

The requirement that the Parties act 'in a spirit of mutual trust and co-operation' is in accordance with a recommendation of Sir Michael Latham in his report on the UK construction industry ('Constructing the Team', July 1994).

Identified and defined terms **11**

11.1   The Contract Data is used to complete the contract by identifying terms in italics and providing the information that certain clauses state is in the Contract Data (see examples A2, B1 and C3).

11.2   The meanings of all defined terms are given in this clause.

11.2(1)   Any departure from the *service* as specified in the contract constitutes a Defect. This includes departures from the work described in Task Orders as well as departures from the Service Information document.

11.2(2)   Defined Cost is defined in this clause in terms of payments made by the *Contractor*. The term is used mainly for assessing certain compensation events (subclause 63.2).

11.2(4)   Prices may comprise both lump sums and measured items.

11.2(5)   One use of this definition of "Provide the Service" in conjunction with the "Service Information" (11.2(6)) is to establish the *Contractor*'s main obligation in subclause 20.1.

11.2(6)   The Service Information is the *Employer*'s statement of what the *Contractor* is required to do in Providing the Service and what constraints the *Contractor* must comply with (subclause 20.1). The Service Information document provided with the invitation to tender will be the basis of the *Contractor*'s tender and must be as comprehensive as possible (see notes on Service Information under 'Stage A: How an *Employer* invites tenders for a job').

The definition includes not only material contained in the document called "Service Information" but also instructions issued under the terms of the contract. This will therefore include Task Orders issued during the course of the contract. The *Employer* may instruct a change to the Service Information document or a Task Order issued under subclause 14.6; this may then be a compensation event (subclause 60.1(1)).

11.2(7) The work to be carried out by the *Contractor* in Providing the Service normally consists of two parts.

The first part is the service detailed in the Service Information document and priced in Part 1 of the Price List. The work in this part does not normally require any specific instructions from the *Employer* e.g. sweep the pavements in the High Street four times per day. But other parts of the work may be described in the Service Information document in generic terms since the precise location and timing may not be known at the start of the *service period* e.g. repair potholes in the carriageways. This work may require specific instructions from the *Employer* say, as to location, as and when the work is required. The work so instructed is paid for on a remeasurable basis under Part 1 of the Price List. Such work does not require the detailed instructions including starting and completion dates of the Task Order system.

The second part is the work instructed on a Task by Task basis as and when the *Employer* requires it. These instructions are issued in the form of Task Orders and are priced at the rates and prices in the Price List which contains the expected quantities of such work. Any Task is limited to "work within the *service*". It is important therefore that the "*service*" is drafted in the Contract Data sufficiently widely to include all types of work likely to be instructed by the *Employer* under the system of Task Orders. A Task may be regarded as a "mini-project" which requires greater management in terms of timing, programming and delay damages.

11.2(8) The specific work comprising a Task Order must have a starting date and a completion date and other information as stated in subclause 14.7. A standard Task Order form is included in the contract. The procedure begins with the *Employer* sending to the *Contractor* the instruction which he is proposing to issue. This is priced by the *Contractor* and sent to the *Employer* with the programme he is proposing, to carry out the Task. When the details are agreed, the *Employer* indicates his acceptance and instructs the *Contractor* to carry out the Task.

11.2(9) The Task Completion Date may be changed when a compensation event occurs affecting the Task.

The Law 12

12.3 Orally agreed changes to the contract have no effect unless they are followed up by the procedures stated in this subclause.

Communications 13

13.2 The *period for reply*, stated in the Contract Data (example A2), aims to achieve a timely turn round of communications. Its length depends on the particular circumstances of the contract but would normally be two or three weeks. Other periods for specific actions are stated in the relevant clauses e.g. subclause 62.1 – submission of quotations for compensation events. All such periods can be changed only by agreement between the Parties.

The *Employer*'s authority, delegation and *Employer*'s Agent 14

14.1 Various clauses in the contract give the *Employer* authority to issue instructions to the *Contractor*. These instructions should be given within the limits and for the reasons expressly stated. If for any reason the *Contractor* disagrees with an instruction, having exhausted the procedures in the contract for dealing with such a situation, his remedy is to follow the dispute resolution procedure in clause 93 as appropriate. He should not refuse to obey the instruction.

14.2 Only the *Employer*, or an authorised delegate or agent of the *Employer* (subclause 14.4), can change the Service Information.

	14.3	This subclause makes clear that acceptance by the *Employer* of the *Contractor*'s communication or his work does not result in a transfer of liability.

14.4   Some employers may wish to delegate many of their actions from the start of the contract, for example to an engineer or facilities manager. If this is the case, the instructions to tenderers should state who the expected delegate is and which actions are likely to be delegated.

14.5   A corporate body may wish to appoint an individual, either from within its own organization or an external consultant to act as its agent under the contract. The *Employer*'s *Agent* may be identified in the Contract Data or appointed some time after the start of the contract.

14.6   A proposed Task Order is drafted by the *Employer* giving details of the Task and is submitted to the *Contractor* for pricing. The *Contractor* prices the Task Order and submits it to the *Employer* together with a Task Order programme, for the *Employer*'s acceptance. A standard Task Order form is included in the contract.

14.7   The delay damages to be included in a Task Order are the amount to be paid by the *Contractor* to the *Employer* if the *Contractor* fails to complete the Task by the Task Completion Date. Under the law of England and Wales, the amount of delay damages should not exceed a genuine pre-estimate of the damage that would be suffered by the *Employer* as a result of the delay to completion. The Parties should consult and seek to agree the amount of delay damages for each Task Order.

Employer provides right of access and things   **15**

15.1 & 15.2   The *Employer* is required to provide the legal right of access to areas affected by the work to be done under the contract. He may not be required to provide the physical access to these areas which may be occupied by people other than the *Employer*. But anything the *Employer* is to provide must be stated in the Service Information, and failure to provide it constitutes a compensation event, subclause 60.1(2).

Early warning   **16**

16.1   The obligation which this clause requires of both Parties is intended to bring into the open as early as possible any matter which could adversely affect the successful outcome of the contract. Both Parties should give early warning in order to maximise the time available for taking avoiding action.

16.2   The Parties are required to co-operate in giving priority to solving the problem, irrespective of how the problem has been caused and who carries financial responsibility for it. Any discussion between the Parties should concentrate on solving the problem. The purpose of the Parties' discussions is not to decide responsibility or who will pay for the actions taken; the relevant provisions of the contract will cover these aspects quite adequately.

2 The *Contractor*'s main responsibilities

Providing the Service   **20**

20.1   This subclause states the *Contractor*'s basic obligation. "Provide the Service" is defined in subclause 11.2(5). It includes supplying all necessary resources to achieve the end result. It demonstrates the importance of thoroughly prepared and comprehensive Service Information (see notes on Service Information under 'Stage A: How an *Employer* invites tenders for a job').

Subcontracting and people **21**

21.1 & As in other NEC contracts, the TSSC does not provide for nominated
21.2 subcontractors. The *Contractor* has full responsibility for Providing the
Service, whether subcontracted or not (see notes on Service Information
under 'Stage A: How an *Employer* invites tenders for a job').

21.3 The *Employer* has authority to have a *Contractor*'s employee removed from
work on the contract. Possible reasons for exercising this authority may
include

- security
- health and safety
- disorderly behaviour affecting the *Employer*'s activities.

3 Time

Starting and the **30**
service period 30.1 The *starting date* and the *service period* are stated in the Contract Data. If
the procurement process and appointment of the *Contractor* takes longer
than anticipated, it may be necessary to adjust the *starting date* by agreement before the Contract Date. If a Task Completion Date occurs after the
end of the *service period* whether because of the date stated in the Task
Order or as a result of a compensation event, the period of the *Contractor*'s
obligation to Provide the Service is extended accordingly.

Instructions to stop or not **31**
to start work 31.1 This subclause gives the *Employer* authority to control the stopping and re-
starting of work for any reason, for example, where there is a risk of injury
to people or damage to property. An instruction given under this subclause
constitutes a compensation event (subclause 60.1(3)). But if it arises
from a fault of the *Contractor*, the Prices are not changed, and in the case
of a Task, the Task Completion Date is not changed. In certain circumstances, if the *Employer* fails to instruct the re-start of work within eight
weeks of instructing work to stop, the *Contractor* may be entitled to terminate (subclause 90.4).

The *Contractor*'s plan **32**
32.1 The *Employer*'s requirements for the *Contractor*'s plan should be stated in
the Service Information (see notes on Service Information under 'Stage A:
How an *Employer* invites tenders for a job'). Some Employers may require
tenderers to submit a plan with their tenders. The *Contractor*'s plan is an
important document for administering the contract. It informs the *Employer*
of the *Contractor*'s detailed intentions of how he is to Provide the Service. It
enables the *Employer* to monitor the *Contractor*'s performance and to
assess the effects of compensation events.

4 Testing and Defects

Tests and inspections   **40**

40.1   The Service Information should include a comprehensive specification of the standards to be achieved for both work and materials.

Any specific requirements of the *Employer* for inspection and testing should be stated in the Service Information, including the associated procedures and responsibilities for carrying out the tests (see notes on Service Information under 'Stage A: How an *Employer* invites tenders for a job').

Where payment for work on its completion is dependent on a test being successful, the description of the item in the Price List should include a reference to the test stated in the Service Information. Where appropriate, separate items may be included in the Price List for carrying out tests which are the *Contractor*'s responsibility.

Notifying Defects   **41**

41.1   The definition of a Defect (subclause 11.2(1)) is based entirely on the Service Information which includes Task Orders. If the *Employer* is not satisfied with work for a reason other than that it is not in accordance with the Service Information or Task Order, the work would not be a Defect. In order to 'correct' the work, the *Employer* would need to instruct a change to the Service Information or Task Order, and this would be a compensation event (subclause 60.1(1)).

Correcting Defects   **42**

42.1   There is no fixed time within which the *Contractor* is required to correct a Defect or make good an omission. This will depend on the circumstances of each particular case. The test to be applied in each case is "Within what time will the Defect or omission and its correction or making good, cause the minimum adverse effect on the *Employer* or others?"

Accepting Defects   **43**

43.1   Although a Defect may be minor, its correction may be costly to the *Contractor*. Correction of the Defect may also cause inconvenience to the *Employer* out of all proportion to the benefits gained. Correction of the Defect may even have become impossible because of the passage of time or some other reason. This subclause states a procedure within the contract for accepting a Defect in these circumstances. Either the *Contractor* or the *Employer* may propose that the Defect should be accepted. The other is not obliged to accept the proposal.

The *Contractor*'s quotation will show a reduction to the Prices. In some cases the reduction may be nominal. If the quotation is not accepted by the *Employer* no further action is necessary other than correction of the Defect.

5 Payment

Assessing the amount due   **50**

50.1   The *Employer*'s statement in the Contract Data fixes an *assessment day* in each month from the *starting date* until the month after the later of the end of the *service period* and the latest date for completion of a Task. This provides for a monthly assessment by the *Contractor* even when the amount due may be nil.

The *Contractor* assesses the amount due by each *assessment day* and uses the assessment to apply to the *Employer* for payment. The "amount due" is the total payment due to date. The *Contractor*'s application for payment is for the change in the amount due since the last payment.

50.2   The payment mechanism is largely based on the use of the Price List and the Prices.

The Price List included in the contract provides the pricing information needed for assessing the amount due. Notes on how to use the Price List are included under its heading in the TSSC and are repeated in these notes under 'Stage A:

How an *Employer* invites tenders for a job'.

The Prices are defined in subclause 11.2(4). The second sentence of the definition provides for the pricing of those items for which a quantity and a rate are stated in the Price List.

Payments for an item in the Price List do not become due until the work described in the item has been completed unless a quantity and a rate are stated, in which case only the Price for the quantity of work completed is included.

Part 1 of the Price List provides for flexibility in tendering methods including items which

    a) the *Employer* describes and for which the tenderer quotes a Price,
    b) the *Employer* describes with a quantity and for which the tenderer quotes a rate extended to a Price (adjustable to quantity completed),
    c) the *Employer* describes and the tenderer breaks down into sub-items comprising a mixture of a) and b), each of which the tenderer quotes for,
    d) the *Employer* describes and the tenderer quotes for a list of the activities necessary to complete the item, each with a Price, or
    e) the tenderer describes and quotes Prices or rates in accordance with the notes at the head of the Price List and the invitation to tender.

The *Employer* should include in the invitation to tender any constraints on how the Price List should be used for the submission of tenders.

It is important that item descriptions are carefully written with appropriate references to the Service Information, including testing requirements. For measured items, the work to be covered by the rate must be clearly stated. If there is a risk of differing interpretations on how an item is measured, the basis of measurement should be included in the item description of the Price List.

The fourth and fifth bullets in subclause 50.2 refer to other amounts to be added or deducted in order to calculate the amount due. Amounts added may include interest on late payments and deductions may include such things as delay damages.

It is recommended that the Parties should agree, at the start of the contract, how the administration of sales tax documentation should be dealt with as part of the payment procedure.

No provision is made for inflation. In some countries where inflation is high the *Employer* may wish to take the risk of price increases beyond a predetermined threshold. This could be provided for in additional conditions of contract.

No provision has been made for advanced payments. If the *Employer* is prepared to make an advanced payment, a separate item should be included in the Price List. The item must describe how the advanced payment is repaid.

This subclause should be read in conjunction with subclause 51.2 with respect to late payments.

Payment 51

51.1 The latest date for payment is related to the assessment day which occurs after the *Employer* receives the *Contractor*'s application.

51.2 For simplicity, a fixed rate of interest of 0.5% per week is stated for the calculation of interest due on late payments, with an option for the *Employer* to state a different rate in the Contract Data.

> Insert a rate only if a rate less than 0.5% per week of delay has been agreed

6 Compensation events

Compensation events 60

As in other NEC contracts, compensation events are those events stated in the contract to be compensation events. If an event is not so stated, it is not a compensation event and is at the *Contractor*'s financial risk. If a compensation event occurs and does not arise from the *Contractor*'s fault, the *Contractor* may be compensated for any effect the event has on cost or in the case of a Task, on the Task Completion Date.

60.1 Events which are compensation events in the TSSC are listed in this subclause. Any additional compensation events required for a particular contract should be stated in an additional condition of contract in the Contract Data.

60.1(1) This subclause embodies the principle that a tender can only be based on the information the tenderer has when the tender is prepared. The exception is the case when the *Employer* is willing to accept a Defect and has agreed to change the Service Information to accommodate it. Service Information as defined in subclause 11.2(6) comprises the document called "Service Information" together with any instructions issued under the contract. The latter include Task Orders. Hence a change to a Task Order is a compensation event under this subclause.

60.1(2) This relates to the *Employer*'s obligation in subclause 15.1 to provide the necessary right of access. It also includes the failure of the *Employer* to provide other things as stated in the Service Information (subclause 15.2).

60.1(3) This subclause relates to the *Employer*'s authority in subclause 31.1 to stop or not to start work.

60.1(4) This relates to the *Employer*'s obligation in subclause 13.2 to reply to a communication within stated periods.

60.1(5) The *Employer* is able to change a decision made under the contract.

Any compensation events other than those identified in subclause 60.1 that are required for a specific contract should be stated in an additional condition of contract in the Contract Data. For example, if there is a significant risk of an increase in the cost of labour due to changes in the law, the occurrence of such a change could be made a compensation event. Any risk which it is prudent for the *Employer* to carry can be dealt with in this way.

Notifying compensation events **61**

61.1 Either the *Employer* or the *Contractor* can notify a compensation event to the other; this subclause limits when the *Contractor* can do so. The *Employer* would normally instruct the *Contractor* to submit a quotation at the same time as notifying the *Contractor* of a compensation event.

The stated time limit is intended to expedite the procedure so that dealing with compensation events a long time after they have occurred is avoided.

61.2 This subclause states the actions to be taken by the *Employer* within one week of a compensation event being notified by the *Contractor*. If the *Employer* decides that a notified event is not a compensation event, the compensation event procedure does not continue. The *Contractor* may then decide to refer the decision to the *Adjudicator*.

Quotations for compensation events **62**

62.1 This subclause describes what a quotation for a compensation event is to comprise and states the periods within which the *Contractor* is required to submit it. Where a compensation event affects a Task Completion Date in that it is critical to the programmed completion of the Task, the *Contractor* should include in his quotation an appropriate revised Task Completion Date.

Assessing compensation events **63**

Clause 63 states how the effects of compensation events on the Prices are assessed. This is the same whether the assessment is done by the *Contractor*, the *Employer* or the *Adjudicator*.

63.1 This subclause describes the assessment procedure used when the compensation event affects only the quantities of work to be done under items in the Price List for which a quantity and rate are stated. For simplicity, the rates in the Price List are used to price the changed quantities.

63.2 This subclause states the procedure used for all other compensation events. The effect of the compensation event on cost is assessed either as recorded, for work already done or as forecast for work yet to be done.

The percentages for overheads and profit quoted in the *Contractor*'s Offer (see notes on 'Stage B: How a tenderer makes an offer' and example B1) are applied to any change in cost due to the compensation event. Each percentage is required to cover all costs and overheads not included in cost as well as an allowance for profit. One percentage is applied to all elements of cost except people. A separate percentage is used for people because this may be at a different level.

63.3 This subclause emphasises the finality of the assessment of compensation events. If the forecast of the effect on cost included in the accepted or notified assessment proves to be wrong when the work is done, the assessment is not changed.

7 Use of equipment and things

The Parties' use of equipment and things **70**

70.1 This subclause prohibits the *Contractor* from using equipment and other things provided by the *Employer* for his own purposes or for purposes other than for Providing the Service.

70.2 This requires the *Contractor* to return to the *Employer* at the end of the *service period* or a later date for completion of a Task, things which have been provided by the *Employer* for the *Contractor*'s use. If the Service Information so states, the *Employer* may take over from the *Contractor* at the end of the *service period* or later date for completion of a Task, things belonging to the *Contractor* which he has used to Provide the Service.

8 Indemnity, insurance and liability

The method of dealing with the *Employer*'s and *Contractor*'s risks used in the TSSC is different to the approach in the TSC.

The *Contractor*'s liability to Provide the Service is stated in the TSSC in subclause 20.1. Certain financial risks, however, constitute compensation events in subclause 60.1. Additional conditions of contract stated in the Contract Data may include further compensation events.

Limitation of liability **80**

This clause deals with the aspects of liability which concern contractors most.

80.1 This concerns the *Contractor*'s liability for loss of and damage to the *Employer*'s property. This would normally be unlimited unless a limit is set as required by this subclause. The amount stated in the Contract Data is generally set at not more than the cover provided by the insurance required in terms of the contract. In effect, the *Contractor* is then only exposed to the amount of the deductible for any one claim.

80.2 This subclause limits the *Contractor*'s exposure to what are commonly referred to as consequential or indirect losses incurred by the *Employer*.

Insurance cover **82**

82.1 The *Contractor*'s responsibility for providing insurances is stated in this clause, which includes the Insurance Table. The duration of insurance cover is from the *starting date* until the end of the *service period* or the latest date for completion of a Task whichever is the later. It is suggested that at the start of the contract the *Contractor* advises his insurer of the possibility that the duration of insurances may need to be extended to cover Tasks which may not be completed until the end of the *service period*.

If the date for completion of a Task is later than the end of the *service period* it is essential that the *Contractor* notifies the insurer accordingly at the time to ensure that the proper insurance cover is in place. This situation may arise as a result of a Task Completion Date or of actual completion of a Task, being later than the end of the *service period*, or of a compensation event affecting a Task which in turn results in an extension of its Completion Date.

The *Employer* is required to state in the Contract Data the extent of the insurances the *Employer* is providing (if any) and the minimum amount of cover for the first, third and fourth insurances in the Insurance Table.

Insurance of equipment is on a value indemnity basis. This is particularly relevant to insurance of equipment as it means that cover is for replacement with equipment of similar age and condition rather than on a "new for old" basis.

With regard to the fourth event in the Insurance Table, employers in many countries are required by law to insure employees for personal injury and death.

The *Employer* should ensure that policies are in joint names including for those insurances procured by the *Employer* for those matters at the *Employer*'s risk.

9 Termination and dispute resolution

Termination and reasons for termination	**90**	
	90.1	The *Employer* is obliged to issue a termination certificate if either Party wishes to terminate in accordance with subclauses 90.2, 90.3, 90.4 or 90.5. The *Contractor* then does no further work.
	90.2 to 90.5	The *Employer* may terminate for any reason (subclause 90.3). The *Contractor* may terminate only for the particular reasons stated.
Procedures on termination	**91**	
	91.1	The *Employer* will secure title to any materials when the *Employer* has paid for them. This will be achieved by the payment on termination (see subclause 92.1). The *Contractor* is required to remove his equipment.
Payment on termination	**92**	
	92.1	This subclause lists the components that are always included in the amount due on termination.
	92.2 & 92.3	These subclauses state further components which are included in the amount due when termination has occurred for particular reasons. They reflect the different reasons for termination.
		Reason 8 is deliberately not mentioned in these subclauses. If Reason 8 is the cause of termination the amount due is only that stated in subclause 92.1.
Dispute resolution	**93**	The simple adjudication procedure provided is designed to be appropriate for the type of work likely to be undertaken under the TSSC. In contracts where the UK Housing Grants, Construction and Regeneration Act 1996 applies, subclause 94.1 replaces subclause 93.3(1), to make the procedure comply with the Act.
	93.1	This subclause establishes the principle, followed in other NEC contracts, that any dispute which cannot be resolved by the Parties themselves must be decided by the *Adjudicator* who is independent of the Parties and is required to act impartially.

The *Adjudicator*   93.2(1)   The person appointed as *Adjudicator* should normally be named in the Contract Data. The *Adjudicator*'s impartiality and independence must be ensured. It is recommended that possible names are suggested by the *Employer* in the invitation to tender so that the *Contractor* can agree a name for inclusion in the final Contract Data (see examples A2 and C3). Acceptance of the *Contractor*'s Offer signifies agreement to the named *Adjudicator*.

The *Adjudicator* should be a person with practical experience of the kind of service to be provided by the *Contractor*. The *Adjudicator* should be able to

- understand the procedures embodied in the TSSC
- understand the roles of both the *Employer* and the *Contractor* in the TSSC
- act impartially and in a spirit of independence of the Parties
- understand and have access to costs at current market rates
- understand and have access to information on planning times and productivities
- appreciate risks and how allowances for them should be set and
- obtain other specialist advice when required.

Under the NEC Adjudicator's Contract the *Adjudicator* is appointed jointly by the Parties. Unless the Parties agree otherwise, his charges (fees and expenses) are shared equally between the Parties, regardless of the *Adjudicator*'s decision on the dispute.

93.2(2)   This subclause makes provision for the appointment of an *Adjudicator* when necessary. This will be because one was not identified in the Contract Data, or the originally chosen *Adjudicator* is no longer able to act. Initially, the Parties should try to reach agreement on a suitable person. If they cannot agree, the *Adjudicator nominating body* named in the Contract Data will make the choice for them. In the UK, the Construction Industry Council and the professional institutions have lists of adjudicators from which the *Adjudicator* may be selected.

The adjudication   93.3(1)   In order to ensure the early declaration of a dispute and expedite its resolution, time limits are stated. After notification of a dispute a minimum of two weeks (maximum four weeks) has to elapse before the dispute can be referred to the *Adjudicator*. This is intended to allow and encourage the Parties to resolve the dispute themselves. Compliance with the time periods stated in this clause is crucially important otherwise the dispute is barred from referral to the *Adjudicator*.

93.3(2) & (3)   These subclauses set time limits for providing information to the *Adjudicator*, and allow the *Adjudicator* to issue any instructions necessary to help him in reaching a decision.

93.3(5)   This requires the *Adjudicator* to use the procedures for assessing compensation events in clause 63 if he has to assess additional cost or delay caused to the *Contractor*.

93.3(6)   The time for the *Adjudicator*'s decision is fixed, but it can be extended if necessary by agreement. If the decision is not given within the time required, and no further time is agreed, a Party can act as though the *Adjudicator* had resigned. This allows the Party to have a replacement *Adjudicator* appointed under subclause 93.2(2).

Review by the *tribunal*   93.4   Under subclause 93.3(8) the *Adjudicator*'s decision is binding unless and until it is revised by the *tribunal*. A dispute cannot be referred to the *tribunal* unless it has first been referred to the *Adjudicator*.

This subclause states the circumstances in which a referral can be made with a time limit for notifying a Party's intention to do so. The *Employer* identifies the *tribunal* in the Contract Data (see example A2). The choice will normally be between arbitration and the courts, either being competent to give a legally final and binding decision on the dispute. It is important to be aware of the different choices that are available when making the decision about the *tribunal.* Different laws and arbitration procedures exist in different countries, whilst in some countries no arbitration exists at all. If the *tribunal* is arbitration, the arbitration procedure to be used is also stated in the Contract Data (see example A2).

94.1   If the United Kingdom Housing Grants, Construction and Regeneration Act 1996 (referred to as 'the Act' in the following notes) applies to the contract, subclause 93.3(1) is replaced by this subclause. It is not necessary to select the changed clause in the Contract Data; the drafting of the clause means that the substitution will be automatic if the Act applies. The Contract Data does however require the *Employer* to state whether or not the Act applies to the contract.

The provisions of subclause 93.3(1) do not comply with the Act although the principle of independent adjudication of disputes has been a key feature of the NEC family since its first publication in 1991. An objective in all NEC contracts is to overcome, where possible, the causes of disputes and, where they still arise, to motivate their clear definition and early resolution.

Subclause 94.1 allows for adjudication 'at any time'. Whilst this does not provide the early certainty that subclause 93.3(1) provides, it has been included to enable the procedure to comply with the Act so that the 'Scheme for Construction Contracts' does not apply.

JOINING SUBCONTRACT DISPUTES WITH MAIN CONTRACT DISPUTES

The following notes apply whether subclause 93.3(1) or subclause 94.1 is used.

Under subclause 21.1, the *Contractor* is responsible for all subcontractors. It is recommended that the *Adjudicator* named in the main contract is also appointed to act in all subcontracts, subject, of course, to the agreement of the subcontractor concerned.

If the *Contractor* wishes to have any matter arising under or in connection with a subcontract that impinges on a main contract matter decided with the main contract matter, the following clause should be included in the main contract.

Combining procedures   93.5

If there is a matter arising under or in connection with a subcontract to this contract which is also a matter arising under or in connection with this contract

- the *Contractor* notifies the subcontractor that the subcontractor may attend the meeting between the Parties or
- the *Contractor* may submit the subcontract matter to the *Adjudicator* at the same time as the main contract matter.

Decisions are made on the two matters together and references to the Parties include the subcontractor.

Stage A   How an *Employer* invites tenders for a job

Example A1   Title page

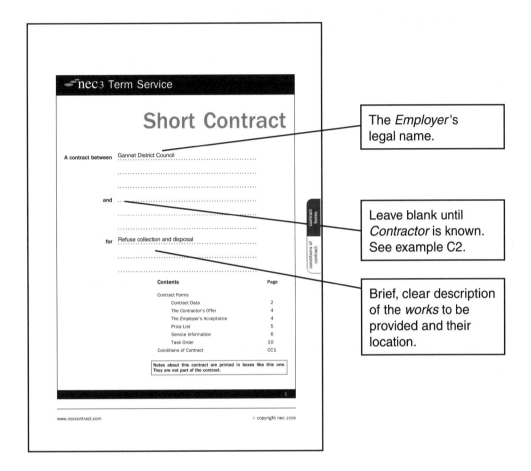

Example A2 Contract Data

The *Employer*'s legal name (as on title page).

Employer's postal address, telephone, E-mail address for the purpose of the contract (not necessarily the registered address).

GN on subclause 14.5.

Description of the *service* (as on title page).

GN on subclause 30.1.

GN on subclause 13.2.

GN on subclause 50.1.

GN on subclause 93 and subclause 94.1

nec 3 Term Service Short Contract

Contract Data

The *Employer* is

Name — Gannet District Council

Address — Council Offices, Lilac Gardens, Suburbia S86 2XY

Telephone — 01234 567890

E-mail address — Contracts@gdc.gov.uk

If the *Employer* appoints an *Employer's Agent*, the *Employer's Agent* is

Name

Address

Telephone

E-mail address

The authority of the *Employer's Agent*, is

The *service* is — Refuse collection and disposal

The *starting date* is — 1 April 2009

The *service period* is — 24 months.

The *period for reply* is — 2 weeks.

The *assessment day* is the — last Monday of each month.

Does the United Kingdom Housing Grants, Construction and Regeneration Act (1996) apply? — Yes / No (delete as appropriate)

© copyright nec 2008

www.neccontract.com

GN on subclause 51.2.

State any insurances which the *Employer* will provide which are included in the Insurance Table. GN on subclause 82.1.

Leave blank if there are suggested names in the invitation to tender; GN on subclause 93.2(1). These are completed when the *Adjudicator* is known.

GN on subclause 80.1.

GN on subclause 82.1, (Insurance Table).

GN on subclause 93.(2).

If the *Employer* requires to include additional conditions of contract they should be inserted in the box provided at the end of the Contract Data. Any additional conditions should be drafted in the same style as the TSSC clauses, using the same defined terms and other terminology. They should be carefully checked, preferably by flowcharting, to ensure that they mesh with the TSSC clauses.

Additional conditions should be used only when absolutely necessary to accommodate special needs which are not covered by the TSSC clauses. Such special needs may be those peculiar to the country where the work is to be done.

See notes on additional compensation events under subclause 60.1.

Many special needs can be accommodated during the invitation to tender, by insertions in the Works Information and by appropriate use of the Price List.

Stage B   How a tenderer makes an offer

Example B1   The *Contractor*'s Offer

The tenderer's legal name.

Tenderer's postal address, telephone and E-mail address for the purpose of the contract.

To be signed by a person having the necessary authority.

Left blank until completed at a later stage by the *Employer*. See example C1

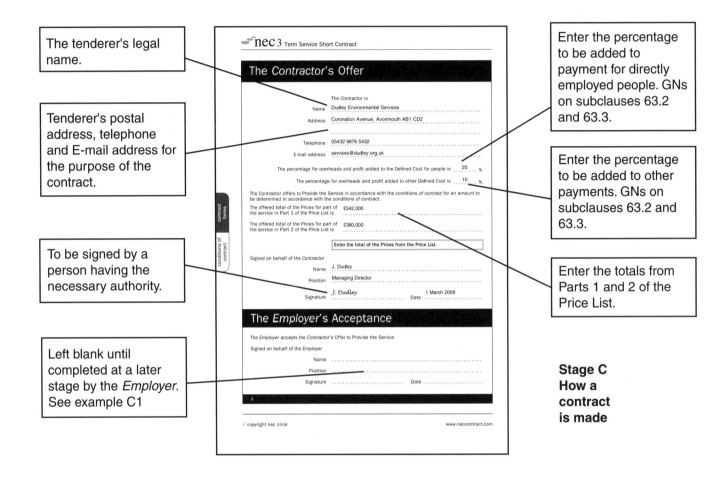

Enter the percentage to be added to payment for directly employed people. GNs on subclauses 63.2 and 63.3.

Enter the percentage to be added to other payments. GNs on subclauses 63.2 and 63.3.

Enter the totals from Parts 1 and 2 of the Price List.

Stage C
How a
contract
is made

Stage C How a contract is made

Example C1 The *Employer*'s acceptance

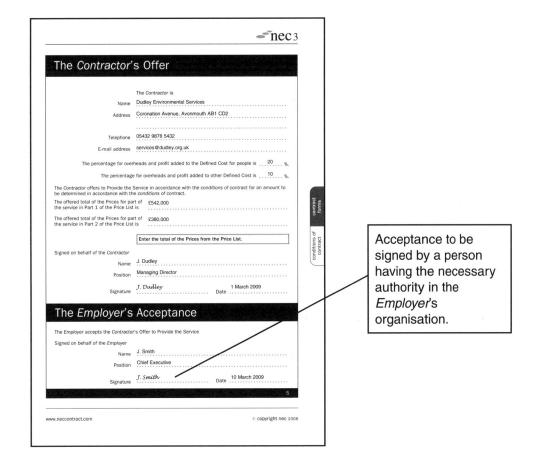

Acceptance to be signed by a person having the necessary authority in the *Employer*'s organisation.

Example C2   Title page

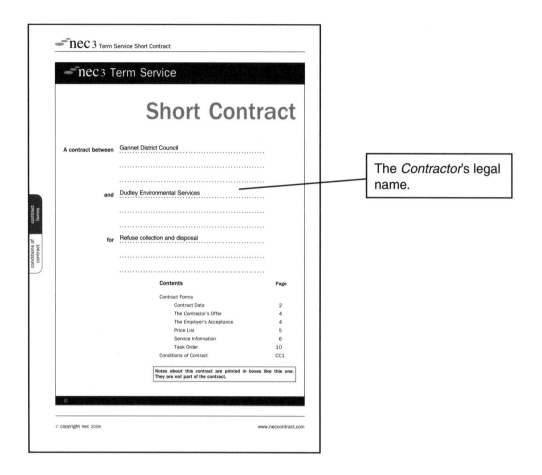

The *Contractor*'s legal name.

Example C3   Contract Data

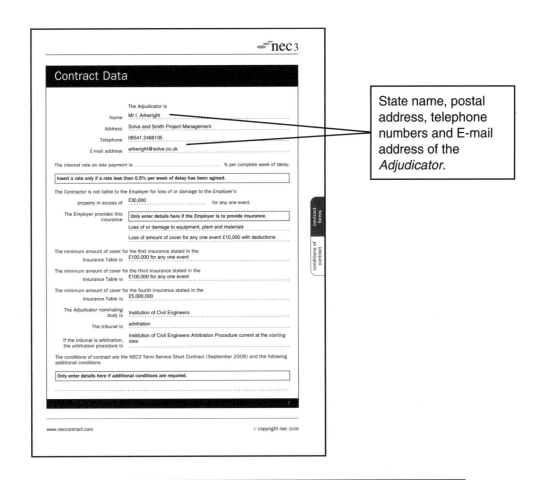

Normally there should be no changes to the second page of the Contract Data unless agreed by the Parties.

MULTI-PARTY PARTNERING

Introduction

A partnering contract, between two Parties only, is achieved by using a standard NEC contract. If partnering is required between two or more parties working on the same project or programme of projects, then amendments are required to the TSSC. In other NEC contracts, secondary Option X12 Partnering is provided to achieve this arrangement. The TSSC does not have a secondary Options structure so a stand alone clause has been drafted using X12 as a basis. This stand alone clause is referred to as the TSSC multi-party partnering clause in this document. This clause can be used alongside other contracts using X12. Similar amendments would be necessary if the multi-party arrangement was to be extended to a subcontractor appointed using the TSSC as a subcontract.

The parties who have the TSSC multi-party partnering clause included in their contracts are all the bodies who are intended to make up the project partnering team. The TSSC multi-party partnering clause does not create a multi-party contract.

This clause does not duplicate provisions of the appropriate existing conditions of contract in the NEC family that will be used for the individual contracts. It follows normal NEC structure in that it is made up of clauses, data and information.

The content is derived from the Guide to Project Team Partnering published by the Construction Industry Council (CIC). The requirements of the CIC document that are not already in the NEC bi-party contract are covered in this clause. The structure of the NEC family of contracts means the TSSC multi-party partnering clause will not work unless an NEC contract is used.

The purpose of this clause (and Option X12 Partnering) is to establish the NEC family as an effective contract basis for multi-party partnering. As with all NEC documents it is intended that the range of application should be wide. By linking this clause (or X12) to appropriate bi-party contracts, it is intended that the NEC can be used for partnering for any number of projects (i.e. single project or multi-project),

- internationally,
- for projects of any technical composition, and
- as far down the supply chain as required.

This clause is given legal effect by including it in the appropriate bi-party contract. It is not a free standing contract but a part of each bi-party contract that is common to all contracts in a project team.

The underlying bi-party contract will be for a contribution of any type, the work content or objective of which is sufficiently defined to permit a conventional NEC contract to be signed.

Parties must recognise that by entering into a contract with the TSSC multi-party partnering clause they will be undertaking responsibilities additional to those in the basic NEC contract.

A dispute (or difference) between Partners who do not have a contract between themselves is resolved by the Core Group. This is the Group that manages the conduct of the Partners in accordance with the Partnering Information. If the Core Group is unable to resolve the issue, then it is resolved under the procedure of the Partners' Own Contracts, either directly or indirectly with the *Client*, who will always be involved at some stage in the contractual chain. The *Client* may seek to have the issues on all contracts dealt with simultaneously.

The TSSC multi-party partnering clause does not include direct remedies between non-contracting Partners to recover losses suffered by one of them caused by a failure of the other. These remedies remain available in each Partner's Own Contract, but their existence will encourage the parties to compromise any differences that arise.

This applies at all levels of the supply chain, as a *Contractor* who is a Partner retains the responsibility for actions of a subcontractor who is a Partner.

The final sanction against any Partner who fails to act as stated in the TSSC multi-party partnering clause is for the Partner who employed them not to invite them to partner again.

Additional Contract Data for the TSSC multi-party partnering clause

The *Client* is the Party for whom the projects are being carried out. He may also be the *Employer* in an NEC contract.

The *Client*'s objective is the objective for the 'programme of projects' if more than one or for 'the project' if only one. The objective should be expressed quantitatively if possible (the business case). It should also include the partnering objectives.

Partnering Information includes any requirements for

- use of common information systems, sharing of offices,
- attendance at Partners' and Core Group meetings,
- participation in partnering workshops,
- arrangements for joint design development,
- value engineering and value management,
- risk management, and
- other matters that the Core Group manages.

This information should not duplicate requirements in the bi-party contracts.

The additional Contract Data for the TSSC multi-party partnering clause, like other Contract Data in the NEC contracts, does not change. The Schedule of Partners and the Schedule of Core Group Members, like the schedules referred to in the Contract Data do change from time to time. The following are samples of the typical information required in these schedules.

Schedule of Partners

Date of last revision: . . . .

The Partners are the following.

Name of Partner	Representative's address and contact details	Contribution and objective	Joining date	Leaving date	Key Performance Indicator	Target	Measurement arrangement	Amount of Payment if the target is improved upon or achieved*

* Enter *nil* in the last column if there is to be no money incentive

Schedule of Core Group Members

Date of last revision: . . . .

The Core Group members are the *Client* and the following.

Name of Partner	Address and contact details	Joining date	Leaving date

Including the TSSC multi-party partnering clause in the Own Contracts

This clause is given legal effect by including it in the appropriate bi-party contract. It is not a free standing contract but a part of each bi-party contract that is common to all contracts in a project team.

The underlying bi-party contract will be for a contribution of any type, the work content or objective of which is sufficiently defined to permit a conventional NEC contract to be signed.

Parties must recognise that by entering into a contract with the TSSC multi-party partnering clause they will be undertaking responsibilities additional to those in the basic NEC contract.

A dispute (or difference) between Partners who do not have a contract between themselves is resolved by the Core Group. This is the Group that manages the conduct of the Partners in accordance with the Partnering Information. If the Core Group is unable to resolve the issue, then it is resolved under the procedure of the Partners' Own Contracts, either directly or indirectly with the *Client,* who will always be involved at some stage in the contractual chain. The *Client* may seek to have the issues on all contracts dealt with simultaneously.

The TSSC multi-party partnering clause does not include direct remedies between non-contracting Partners to recover losses suffered by one of them caused by a failure of the other. These remedies remain available in each Partner's Own Contract, but their existence will encourage the parties to compromise any differences that arise.

This applies at all levels of the supply chain, as a *Contractor who* is a Partner retains the responsibility for actions of a subcontractor who is a Partner.

The final sanction against any Partner who fails to act as stated in the TSSC multi-party partnering clause is for the Partner who employed them not to invite them to partner again.

TSSC multi-party partnering

The TSSC multi-party partnering clause is incorporated into the Own Contract of a Partner as follows.

1. The additional conditions below (referred to as Z1 but should be numbered to suit) would be inserted in the 'additional conditions' provision in the Contract Data.

2. Add the following entry to the Contract Data in each bi-party contract:

    *   The *Client* is

        Name. . . . .

        Address . . . .

        . . . .

    *   The *Client*'s *objective* is . . . .

        . . . .

        . . . .

        . . . .

        . . . .

        . . . .

        . . . .

    *   The Partnering Information is in

        . . . .

        . . . .

        . . . .

        . . . .

TSSC multi-party partnering

Z1: Partnering

Identified and defined terms Z1.1

(1) The Partners are those named in the Schedule of Partners. The *Client* is a Partner.

(2) An Own Contract is a contract between two Partners which includes this clause.

(3) The Core Group comprises the Partners listed in the Schedule of Core Group Members.

(4) Partnering Information is information which specifies how the Partners work together and is either in the documents which the Contract Data states it is in or in an instruction given in accordance with this contract.

(5) A Key Performance Indicator is an aspect of performance for which a target is stated in the Schedule of Partners.

Actions Z1.2

(1) Each Partner works with the other Partners to achieve the *Client*'s *objective* stated in the Contract Data and the objectives of every other Partner stated in the Schedule of Partners.

(2) Each Partner nominates a representative to act for it in dealings with other Partners.

(3) The Core Group acts and takes decisions on behalf of the Partners on those matters stated in the Partnering Information.

(4) The Partners select the members of the Core Group. The Core Group decides how they will work and decides the dates when each member joins and leaves the Core Group. The *Client*'s representative leads the Core Group unless stated otherwise in the Partnering Information.

(5) The Core Group keeps the Schedule of Core Group Members and the Schedule of Partners up to date and issues copies of them to the Partners each time either is revised.

(6) This clause does not create a legal partnership between Partners who are not one of the Parties in this contract.

Working together Z1.3

(1) The Partners work together as stated in the Partnering Information and in a spirit of mutual trust and co-operation.

(2) A Partner may ask another Partner to provide information which he needs to carry out the work in his Own Contract and the other Partner provides it.

(3) Each Partner gives an early warning to the other Partners when he becomes aware of any matter that could affect the achievement of another Partner's objectives stated in the Schedule of Partners.

(4) The Partners use common information systems as set out in the Partnering Information.

(5) A Partner implements a decision of the Core Group by issuing instructions in accordance with its Own Contracts.

(6) The Core Group may give an instruction to the Partners to change the Partnering Information. Each such change to the Partnering Information is a compensation event which may lead to reduced Prices.

(7) The Core Group prepares and maintains a timetable showing the proposed timing of the contributions of the Partners. The Core Group issues a copy of the timetable to the Partners each time it is revised. The *Contractor* changes his programme if it is necessary to do so in order to comply with the revised timetable. Each such change is a compensation event which may lead to reduced Prices.

(8) A Partner gives advice, information and opinion to the Core Group and to other Partners when asked to do so by the Core Group. This advice, information and opinion relates to work that another Partner is carrying out under its Own Contract and is given fully, openly and objectively. The Partners show contingency and risk allowances in information about costs, prices and timing for future work.

(9) A Partner notifies the Core Group before subcontracting any work.

Incentives Z1.4 (1) A Partner is paid the amount stated in the Schedule of Partners if the target stated for a Key Performance Indicator is improved upon or achieved. Payment of the amount is due when the target has been improved upon or achieved and is made as part of the amount due in the Partner's Own Contract.

(2) The *Client* may add a Key Performance Indicator and associated payment to the Schedule of Partners but may not delete or reduce a payment stated in the Schedule of Partners.

Guidance notes on TSSC multi-party partnering clauses

Identified and defined terms

Clause Z1.2 (1)
The point at which someone becomes a Partner is when his Own Contract (which includes the TSSC multi-party partnering clause) comes into existence. They should then be named in the Schedule of Partners, and their representative identified.

Clause Z1.2 (3)
Not every Partner is a member of the Core Group.

Clause Z1.2 (5)
There are two options for subcontractor partners. Either the amount payable cascades down if the schedule allocates the same bonus/cost to the main contractor and subcontractor, or the main contractor absorbs the bonus/cost and does not pass it on.

Working together

Clause Z1.3 (5)
The Core Group organises and holds meetings. It produces and distributes records of each meeting which include agreed actions. Instructions from the Core Group are issued in accordance with the Partner's Own Contract. The Core Group may invite other Partners or people to a meeting of the Core Group.

Clause Z1.3 (8)
The Partners should give advice and assistance when asked, and in addition whenever they identify something that would be helpful to another Partner.

Clause Z1.3 (9)
A subcontractor/subconsultant may be a Partner, but the general policy on this should be decided at the beginning of the Project. The Core Group should advise the Contractor/Consultant at the outset if a subcontractor/subconsultant is to be asked to be a Partner. A subcontractor/subconsultant who the Core group decides should be a Partner should not be appointed if he is unwilling to be a Partner.

Possible alternative incentive KPI

Incentives

Clause Z1.4 (1) (also 'Z1.1 (1) and Z1.3 (3)')
If one Partner lets the others down for a particular target by poor performance, then all lose their bonus for that target. If the *Employer* tries to prevent a target being met, he is in breach of subclause 10.1.

There can be more than one KPI for each partner. KPIs may apply to one Partner, to several partners or to all partners.

An example of a KPI

KPI	Number of days to complete each floor of the building framework
Target	14 days
Measurement	Number of days between removal of falsework from the entire slab and from the slab below
Amount	Main contractor – £5,000 each floor Formwork and concrete sub-contractor – £2,000 each floor Structural designer – £750 each floor

Clause Z1.4 (2)
The *Client* should consult with the other Partners before adding a KPI. The effect on subcontracted work should be noted; adding a KPI to work which is subcontracted can involve a change to the KPI for a subcontractor/subconsultant.

Incentives

KPI ability of *Contractor* to complete repair works correctly first time - only applied to *Contractor*

Target	5%
Measurement	Number of recalls arising from defective or incomplete work expressed as a percentage of the number of repairs completed
Amount	0.05% of relevant component of PSPD for repairs

Flow charts for the

Term Service Short Contract

FLOW CHARTS

PREFACE

These flow charts depict the procedures followed when using the NEC3 Term Service Short Contract (TSSC). They are intended to help people using the TSSC to see how the various TSSC clauses produce clear and precise sequences of action for the people involved.

The flow charts are not part of any contract. Much of the text and many of the words taken from the TSSC itself are abbreviated in the flow charts. The flow charts depict almost all of the sequences of action set out in the TSSC. Many of the sequences interact, and because of this, users of the flow charts will often have to review more than one sheet in order to track the full sequence of actions in one area.

ABBREVIATIONS USED IN THE FLOW CHART BOXES

FC 16	Flow chart for clause 16
E	*Employer*
C	*Contractor*
SC	Subcontractor
CD	Contract Data
CE	Compensation event
SI	Service Information

Legend

CHART START

Start

HEADINGS
> Headings in caps
> provide guidance

HELPFUL HEADING

STATEMENTS
> If a subclause is
> referenced, text
> is from the NEC

Statement
explaining
next step

Subclause or
Statement using part or all of the NEC
text in subclause

LOGIC LINKS
> Links go to right
> and/or downward
> unless shown

QUESTION
> Answer question
> to determine the
> route to follow

Does
this subclause
apply?

YES

NO

SUBROUTINE
> Include another
> flow chart here

FC or
Description

CONTINUATION
> Link to matching
> point(s) on other
> chart sheets

A
sheet 2

B
sheet 2

CHART TITLE
> Chart number,
> title and sheet

Flow chart or Sheet 1 of 2
Description

CONTINUATION

A
sheet 2

B
sheet 2

CHART FINISH

Finish

CHART TITLE

Flow chart or Sheet 2 of 2
Description

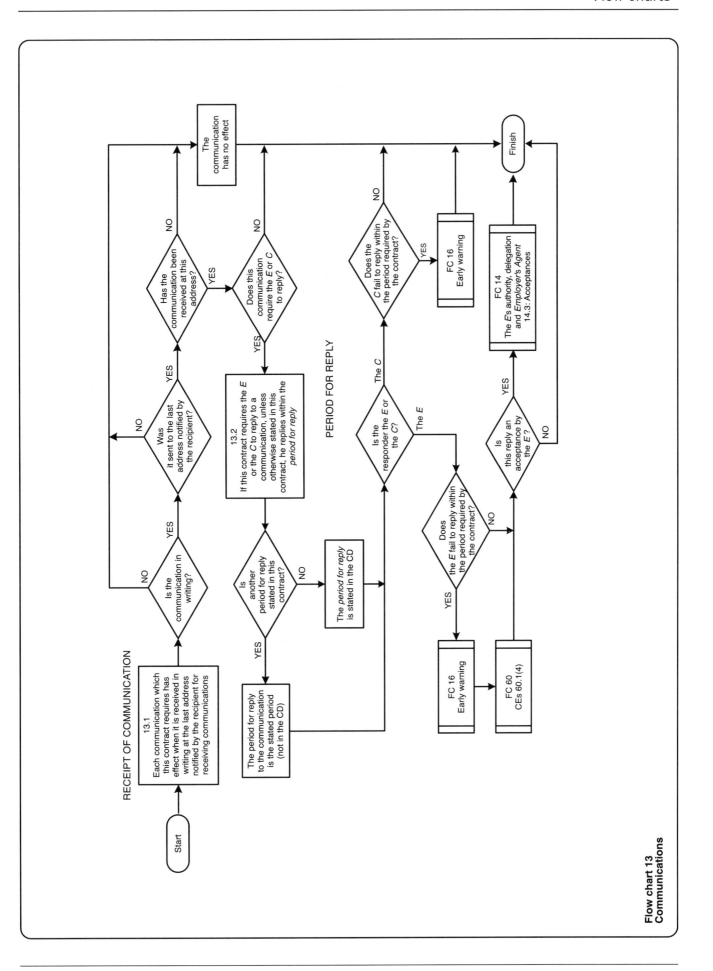

RECEIPT OF COMMUNICATION

PERIOD FOR REPLY

**Flow chart 13
Communications**

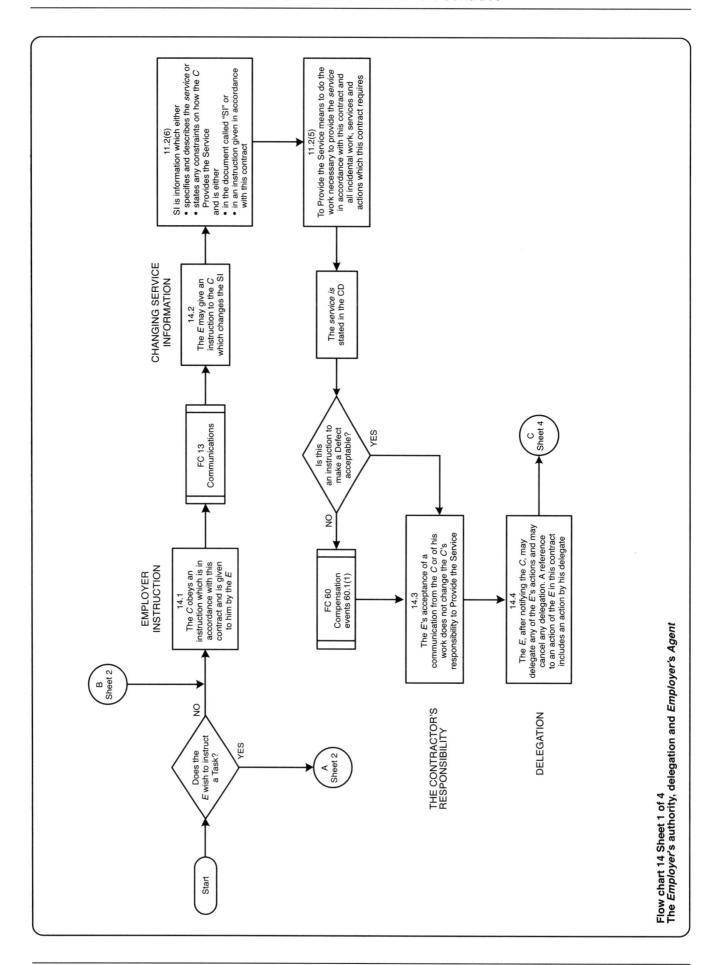

CHANGING SERVICE INFORMATION

11.2(6)
SI is information which either
• specifies and describes the *service* or
• states any constraints on how the *C* Provides the Service
and is either
• in the document called "SI" or
• in an instruction given in accordance with this contract

11.2(5)
To Provide the Service means to do the work necessary to provide the *service* in accordance with this contract and all incidental work, services and actions which this contract requires

14.2
The *E* may give an instruction to the *C* which changes the SI

FC 13
Communications

The *service is* stated in the CD

EMPLOYER INSTRUCTION

14.1
The *C* obeys an instruction which is in accordance with this contract and is given to him by the *E*

Is this an instruction to make a Defect acceptable?

YES

NO

FC 60
Compensation events 60.1(1)

B
Sheet 2

Does the *E* wish to instruct a Task?

NO

YES

A
Sheet 2

Start

THE CONTRACTOR'S RESPONSIBILITY

14.3
The *E*'s acceptance of a communication from the *C* or of his work does not change the *C*'s responsibility to Provide the Service

DELEGATION

14.4
The *E*, after notifying the *C*, may delegate any of the *E*'s actions and may cancel any delegation. A reference to an action of the *E* in this contract includes an action by his delegate

C
Sheet 4

Flow chart 14 Sheet 1 of 4
The *Employer's* authority, delegation and *Employer's Agent*

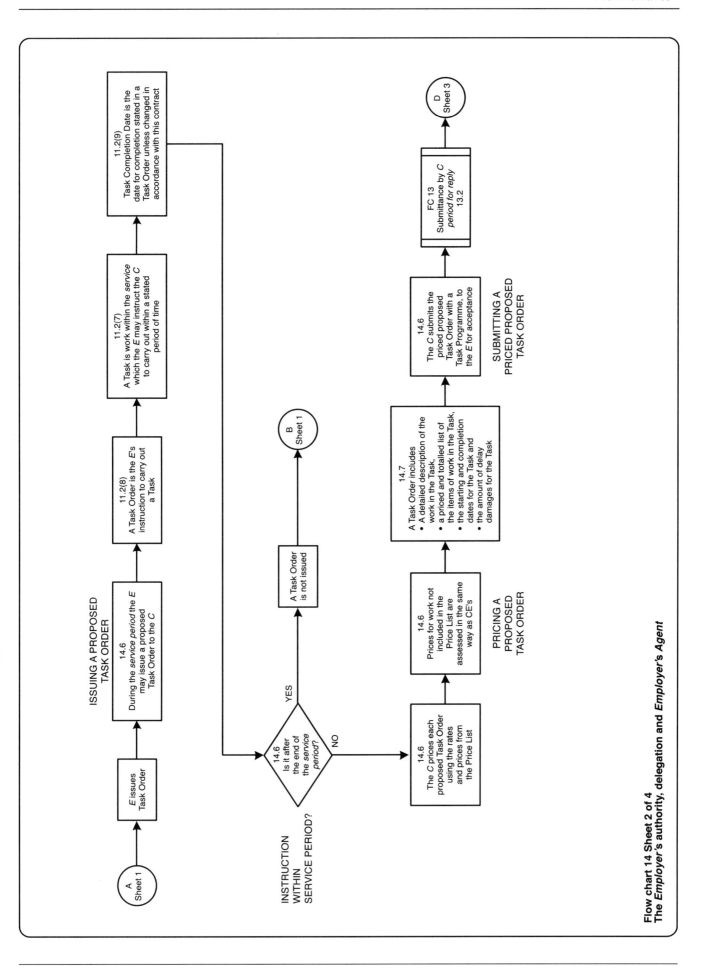

ISSUING A PROPOSED TASK ORDER

A
Sheet 1

E issues
Task Order

14.6
During the *service period* the *E* may issue a proposed Task Order to the *C*

11.2(8)
A Task Order is the *E's* instruction to carry out a Task

11.2(7)
A Task is work within the *service period* which the *E* may instruct the *C* to carry out within a stated period of time

11.2(9)
Task Completion Date is the date for completion stated in a Task Order unless changed in accordance with this contract

INSTRUCTION WITHIN SERVICE PERIOD?

14.6
Is it after the end of the *service period?*

YES → B
Sheet 1

A Task Order is not issued

NO →

14.6
The *C* prices each proposed Task Order using the rates and prices from the Price List

14.6
Prices for work not included in the Price List are assessed in the same way as CE's

PRICING A PROPOSED TASK ORDER

14.7
A Task Order includes
• A detailed description of the work in the Task,
• a priced and totalled list of the items of work in the Task,
• the starting and completion dates for the Task and
• the amount of delay damages for the Task

14.6
The *C* submits the priced proposed Task Order with a Task Programme, to the *E* for acceptance

SUBMITTING A PRICED PROPOSED TASK ORDER

FC 13
Submittance by *C*
period for reply
13.2

D
Sheet 3

Flow chart 14 Sheet 2 of 4
The *Employer's* authority, delegation and *Employer's Agent*

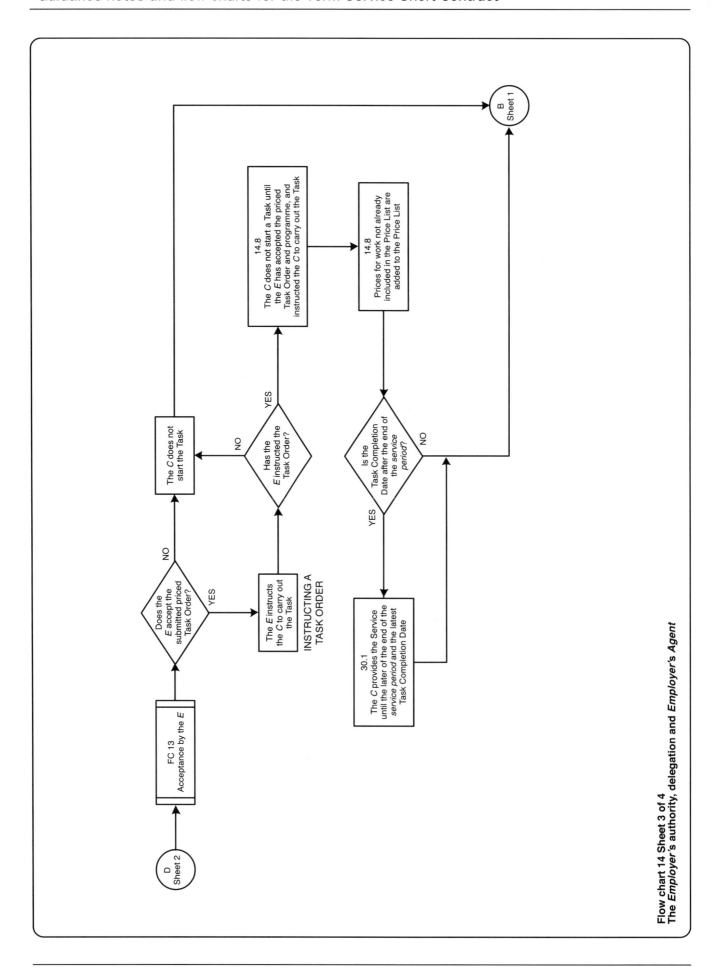

Flow chart 14 Sheet 3 of 4
The *Employer's* authority, delegation and *Employer's Agent*

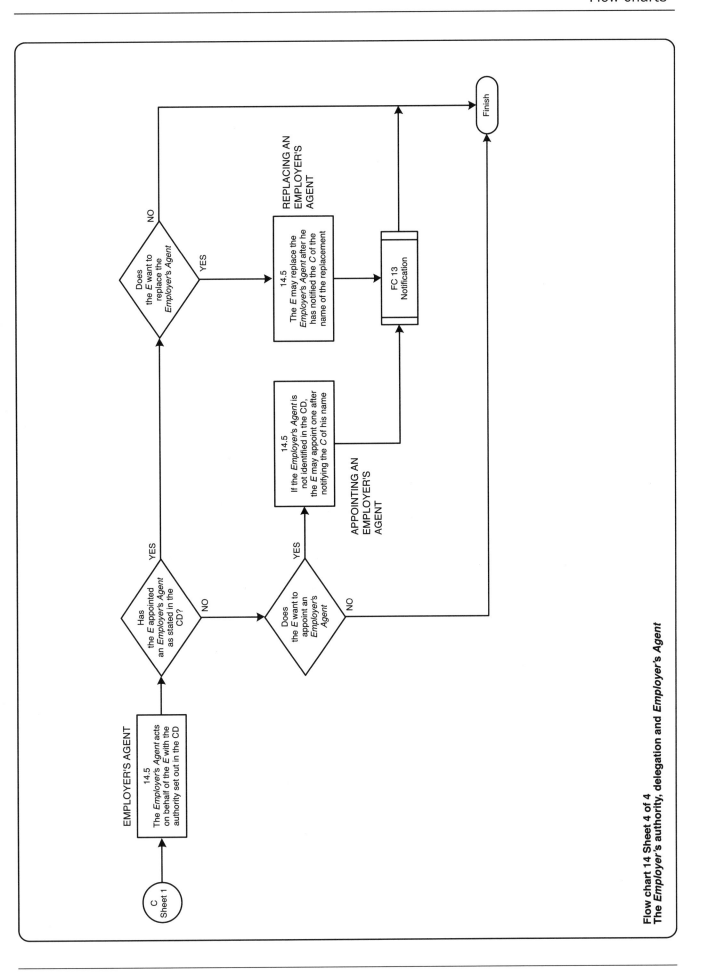

Flow chart 14 Sheet 4 of 4
The *Employer's* authority, delegation and *Employer's Agent*

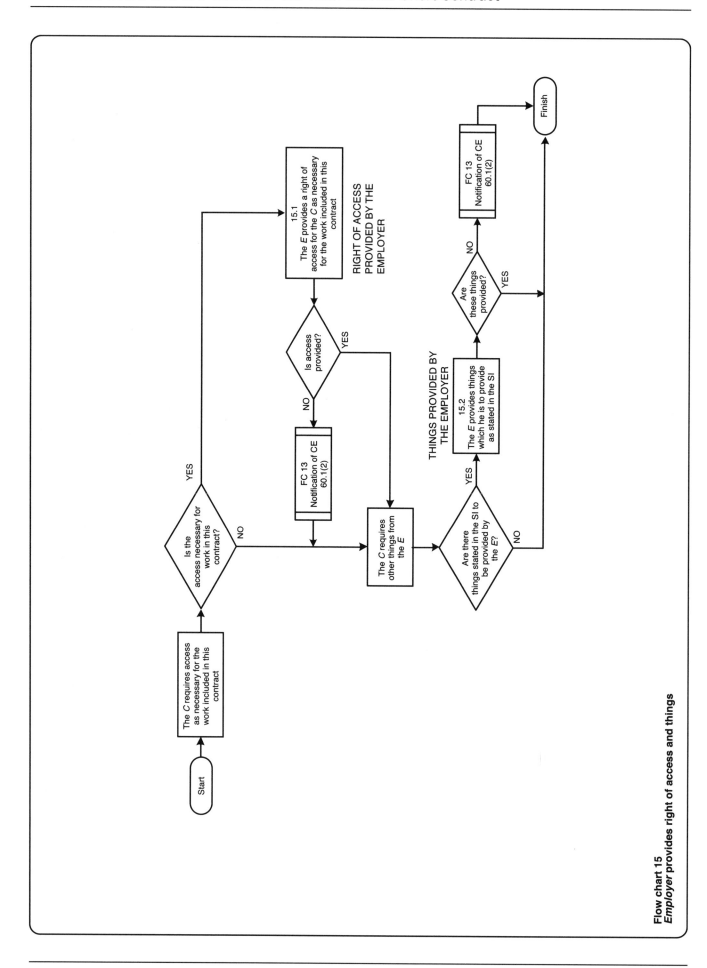

Flow chart 15
Employer **provides right of access and things**

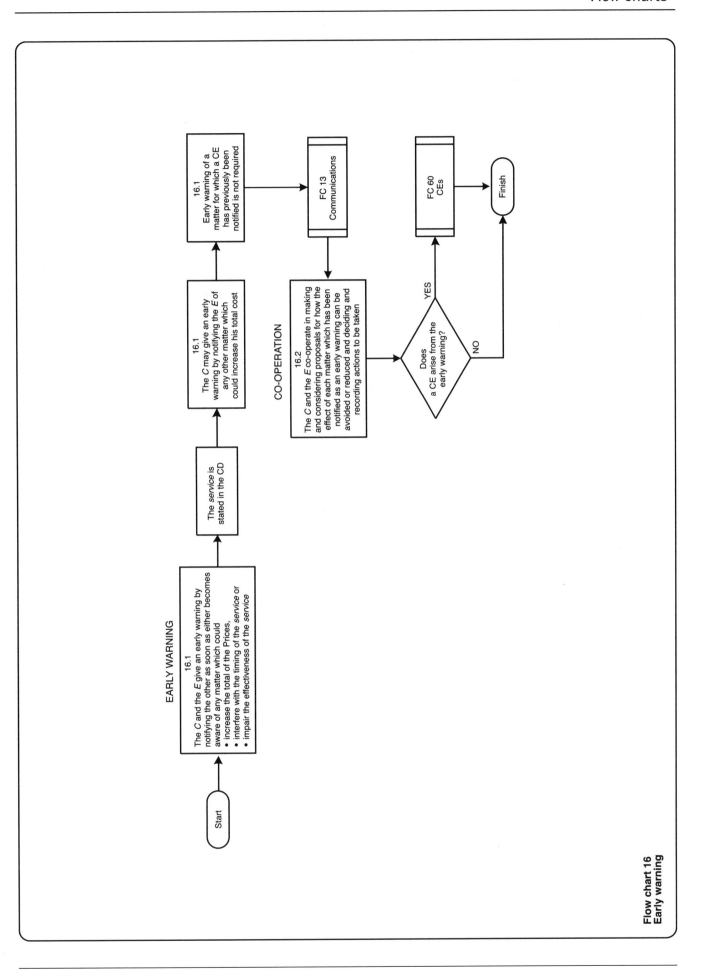

EARLY WARNING

16.1

The *C* and the *E* give an early warning by notifying the other as soon as either becomes aware of any matter which could
• increase the total of the Prices,
• interfere with the timing of the *service* or
• impair the effectiveness of the *service*

The *service* is stated in the CD

16.1

The *C* may give an early warning by notifying the *E* of any other matter which could increase his total cost

16.1

Early warning of a matter for which a CE has previously been notified is not required

FC 13
Communications

CO-OPERATION

16.2

The *C* and the *E* co-operate in making and considering proposals for how the effect of each matter which has been notified as an early warning can be avoided or reduced and deciding and recording actions to be taken

Does a CE arise from the early warning?

YES

NO

FC 60
CEs

Start

Finish

Flow chart 16
Early warning

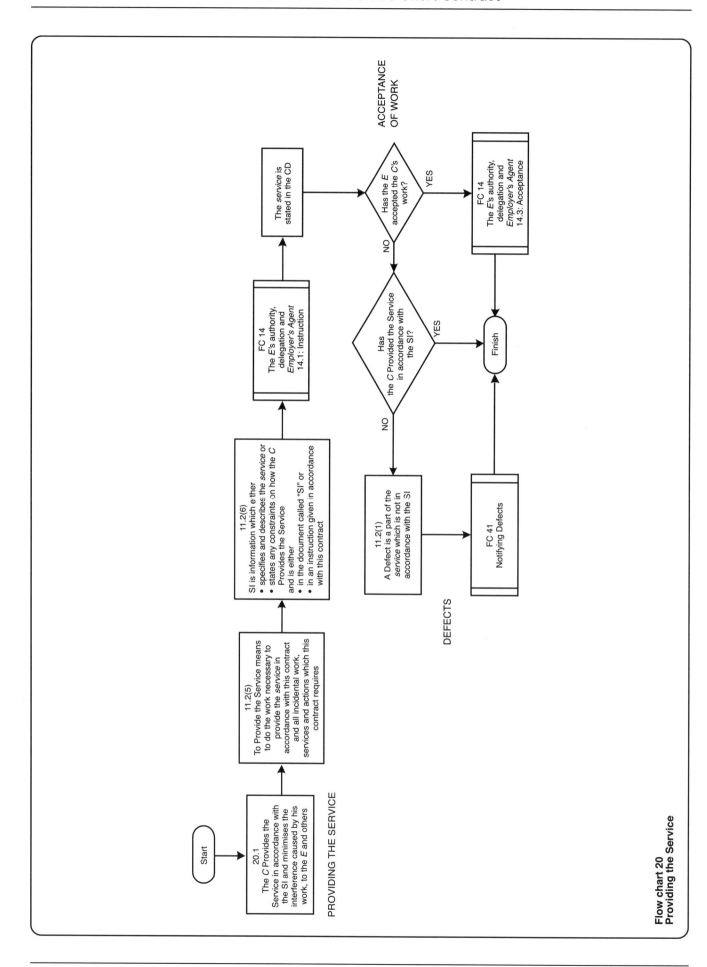

ACCEPTANCE OF WORK

The *service* is stated in the CD

Has the *E* accepted the *C*'s work?

YES → FC 14
The *E*'s authority, delegation and *Employer's Agent*
14.3: Acceptance

NO

FC 14
The *E*'s authority, delegation and *Employer's Agent*
14.1: Instruction

11.2(6)
SI is information which either
• specifies and describes the *service* or
• states any constraints on how the *C* Provides the Service
and is either
• in the document called "SI" or
• in an instruction given in accordance with this contract

Has the *C* Provided the Service in accordance with the SI?

YES → Finish

NO

11.2(1)
A Defect is a part of the *service* which is not in accordance with the SI

FC 41
Notifying Defects

DEFECTS

11.2(5)
To Provide the Service means to do the work necessary to provide the *service* in accordance with this contract and all incidental work, services and actions which this contract requires

20.1
The *C* Provides the Service in accordance with the SI and minimises the interference caused by his work, to the *E* and others

PROVIDING THE SERVICE

Start

Flow chart 20
Providing the Service

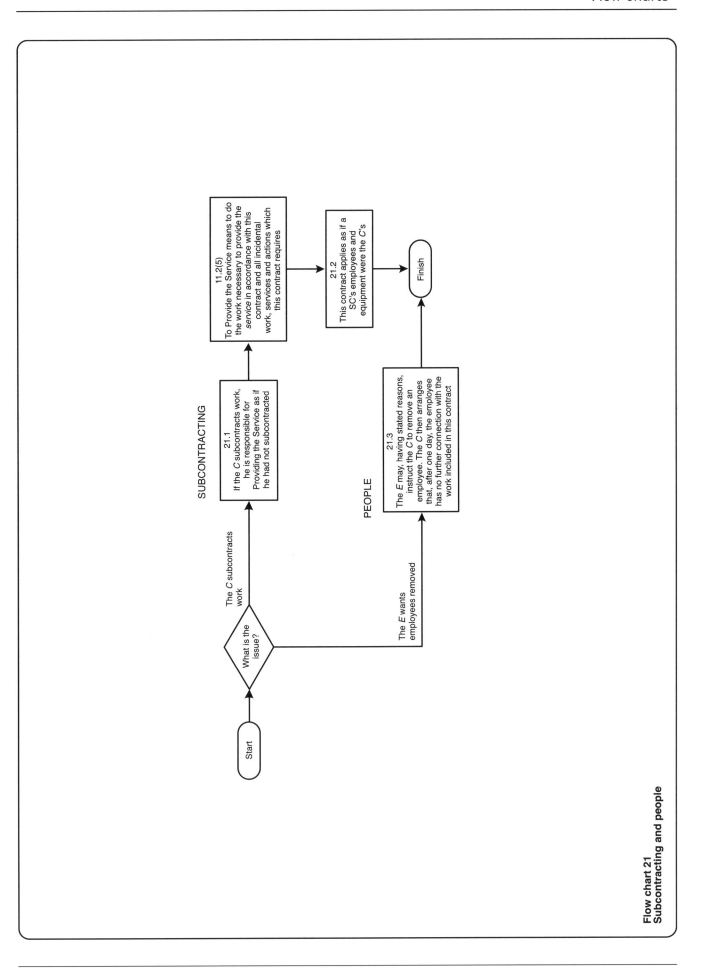

Flow chart 21
Subcontracting and people

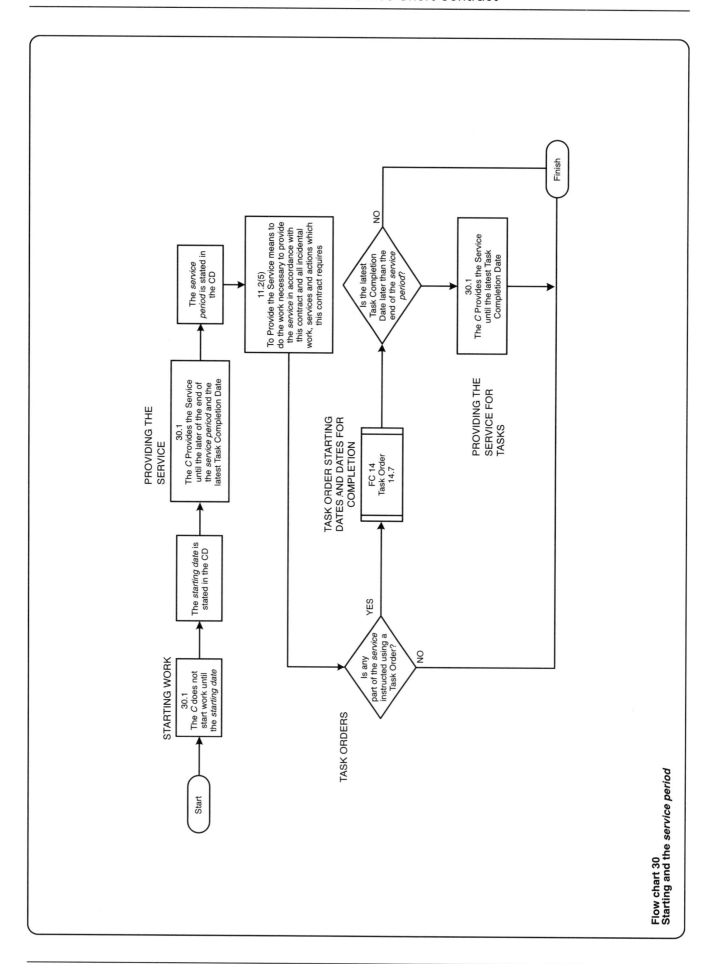

STARTING WORK

Start

30.1
The C does not start work until the starting date

The starting date is stated in the CD

PROVIDING THE SERVICE

30.1
The C Provides the Service until the later of the end of the service period and the latest Task Completion Date

The service period is stated in the CD

11.2(5)
To Provide the Service means to do the work necessary to provide the service in accordance with this contract and all incidental work, services and actions which this contract requires

TASK ORDERS

Is any part of the service instructed using a Task Order?

YES

TASK ORDER STARTING DATES AND DATES FOR COMPLETION

FC 14
Task Order
14.7

Is the latest Task Completion Date later than the end of the service period?

YES

NO

NO

PROVIDING THE SERVICE FOR TASKS

30.1
The C Provides the Service until the latest Task Completion Date

Finish

Flow chart 30
Starting and the service period

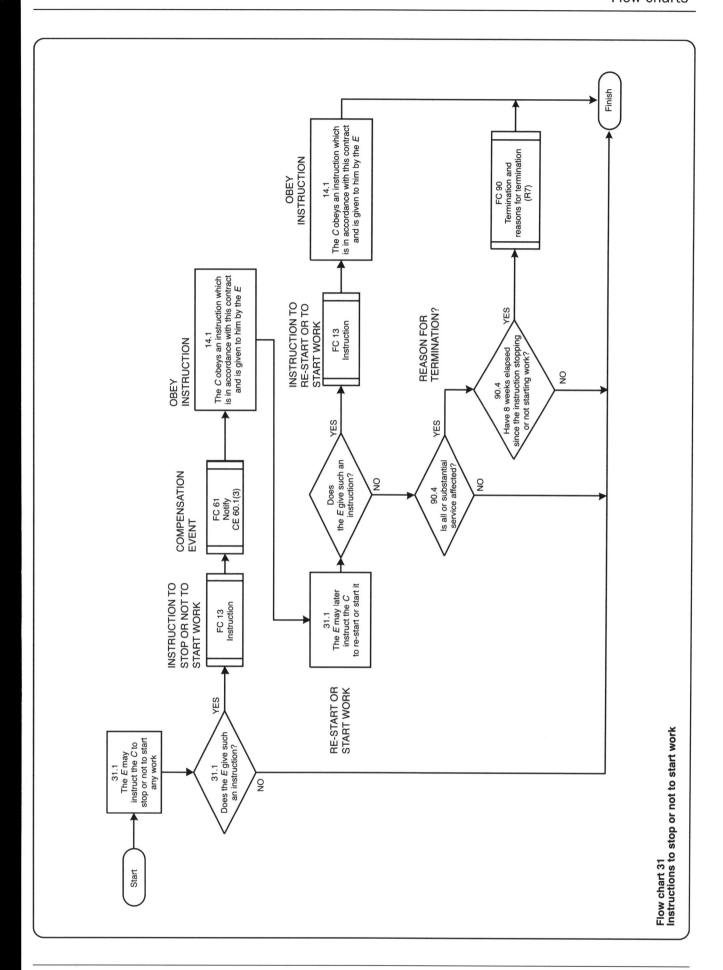

Flow chart 31
Instructions to stop or not to start work

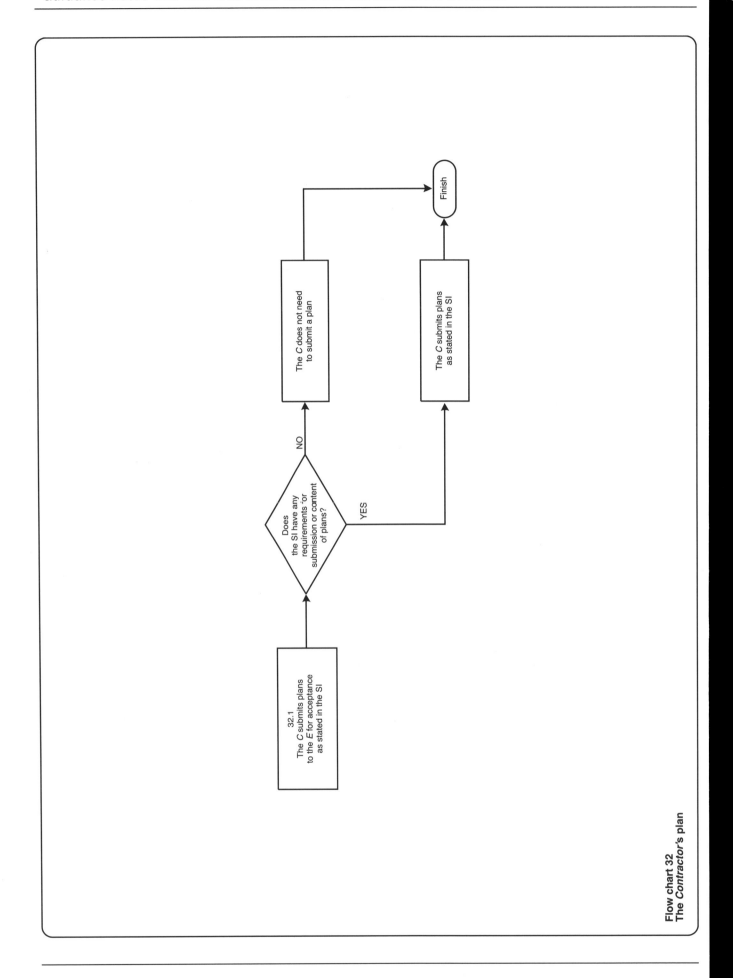

Flow chart 32
The *Contractor*'s plan

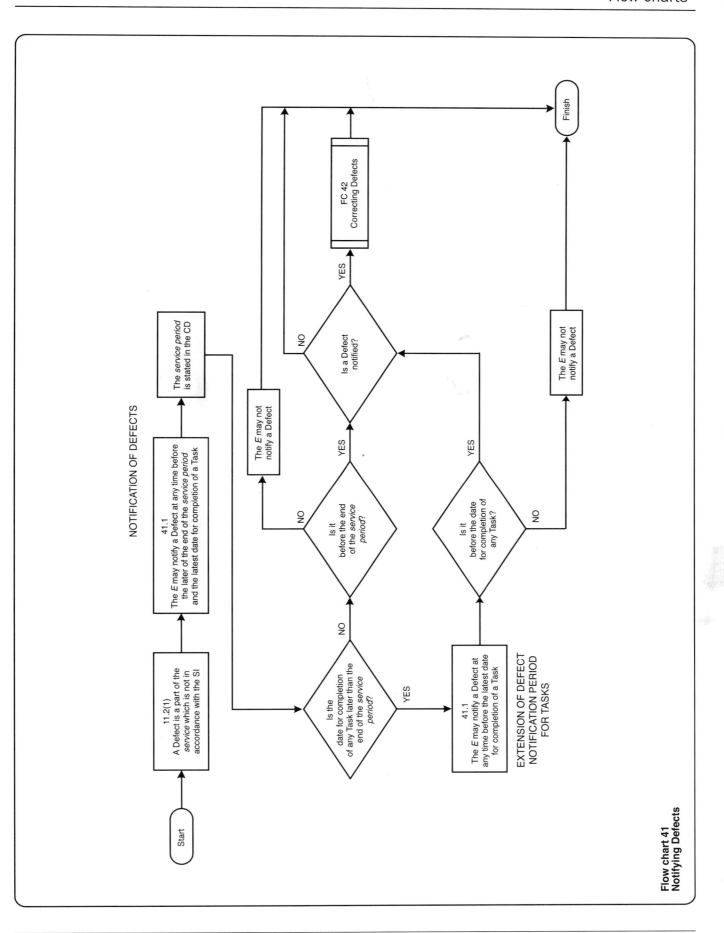

NOTIFICATION OF DEFECTS

Start

11.2(1)
A Defect is a part of the *service* which is not in accordance with the SI

41.1
The *E* may notify a Defect at any time before the later of the end of the *service period* and the latest date for completion of a Task

The *service period* is stated in the CD

Is the date for completion of any Task later than the end of the *service period?*

NO — YES

Is it before the end of the *service period?*

YES — NO

The *E* may not notify a Defect

Is a Defect notified?

NO — YES

FC 42
Correcting Defects

41.1
The *E* may notify a Defect at any time before the latest date for completion of a Task

EXTENSION OF DEFECT NOTIFICATION PERIOD FOR TASKS

Is it before the date for completion of any Task?

YES — NO

The *E* may not notify a Defect

Finish

Flow chart 41
Notifying Defects

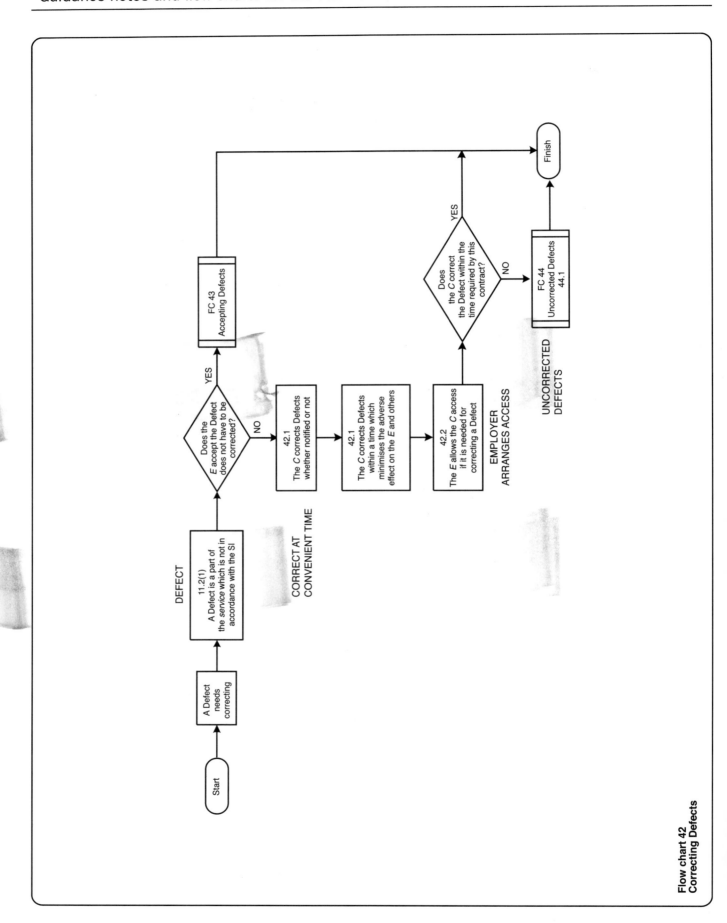

Flow chart 42
Correcting Defects

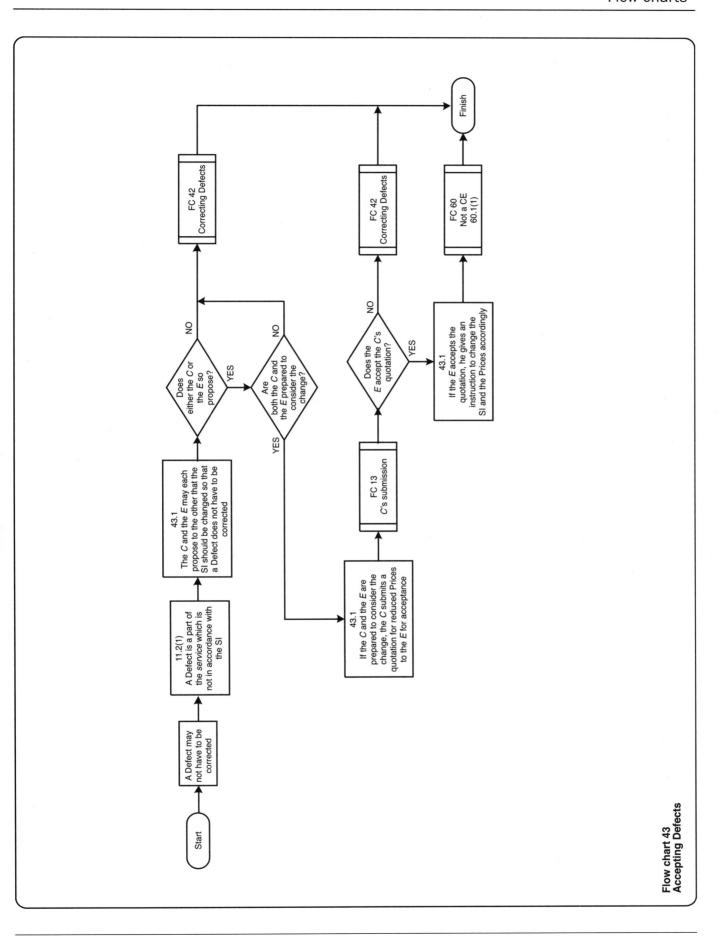

Flow chart 43
Accepting Defects

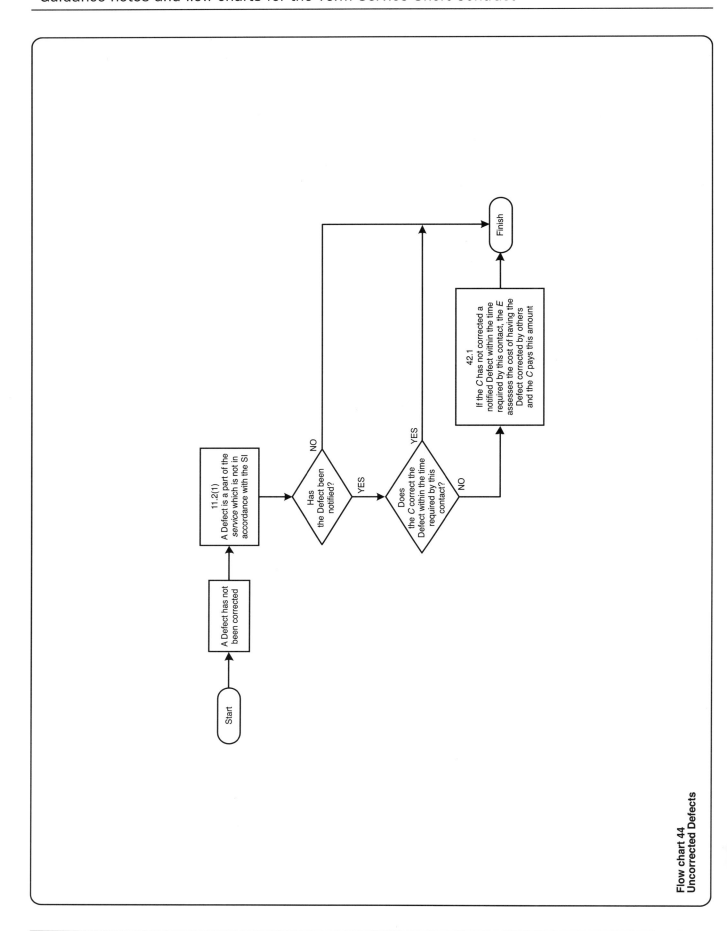

Flow chart 44
Uncorrected Defects

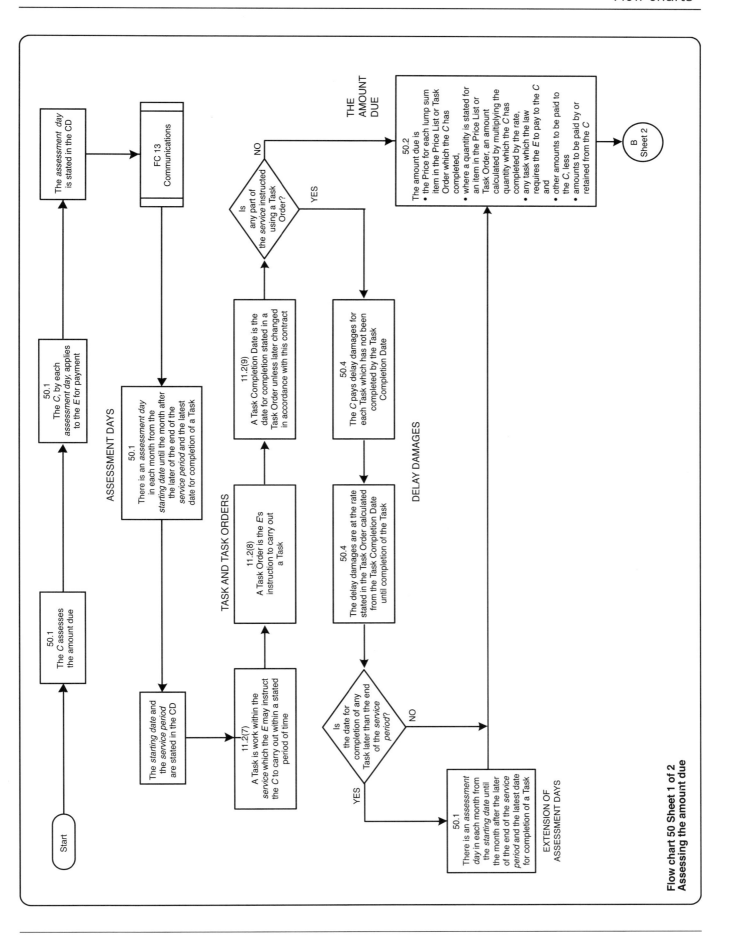

ASSESSMENT DAYS

TASK AND TASK ORDERS

DELAY DAMAGES

EXTENSION OF ASSESSMENT DAYS

THE AMOUNT DUE

Start

50.1
The *C* assesses the amount due

50.1
The *C*, by each *assessment day*, applies to the *E* for payment

The *assessment day* is stated in the CD

FC 13
Communications

50.1
There is an *assessment day* in each month from the *starting date* until the month after the later of the end of the *service period* and the latest date for completion of a Task

The *starting date* and the *service period* are stated in the CD

11.2(7)
A Task is work within the *service* which the *E* may instruct the *C* to carry out within a stated period of time

11.2(8)
A Task Order is the *E*'s instruction to carry out a Task

11.2(9)
A Task Completion Date is the date for completion stated in a Task Order unless later changed in accordance with this contract

Is any part of the *service* instructed using a Task Order?

NO

YES

Is the date for completion of any Task later than the end of the *service period*?

YES

NO

50.1
There is an *assessment day* in each month from the *starting date* until the month after the later of the end of the *service period* and the latest date for completion of a Task

50.4
The *C* pays delay damages for each Task which has not been completed by the Task Completion Date

50.4
The delay damages are at the rate stated in the Task Order calculated from the Task Completion Date until completion of the Task

50.2
The amount due is
• the Price for each lump sum item in the Price List or Task Order which the *C* has completed,
• where a quantity is stated for an item in the Price List or Task Order, an amount calculated by multiplying the quantity which the *C* has completed by the rate,
• any task which the law requires the *E* to pay to the *C* and
• other amounts to be paid to the *C*, less
• amounts to be paid by or retained from the *C*

B
Sheet 2

Flow chart 50 Sheet 1 of 2
Assessing the amount due

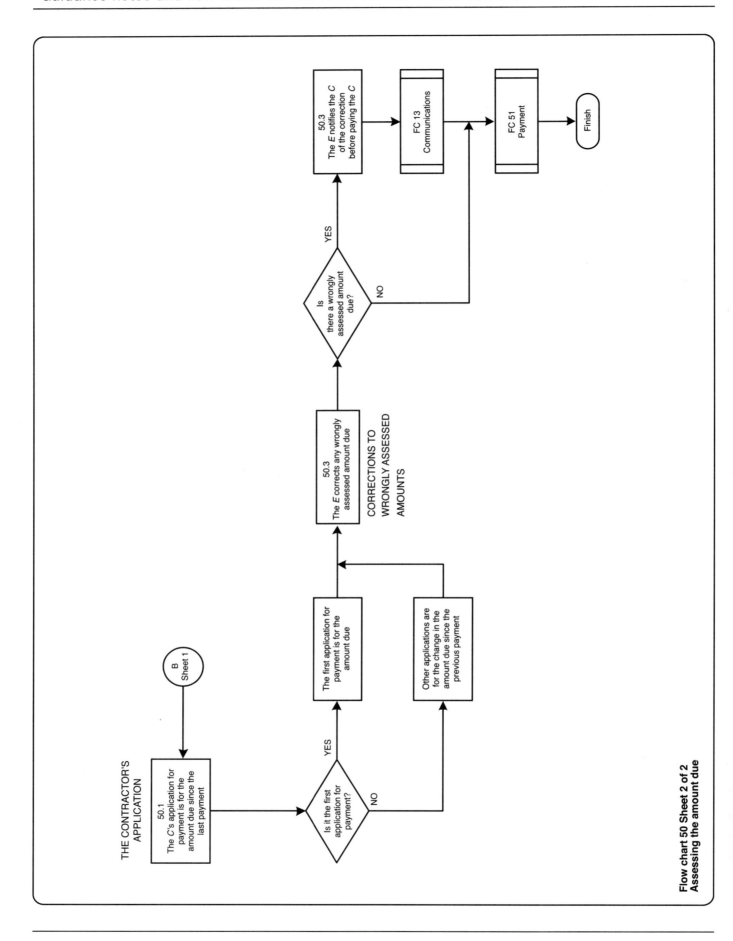

THE CONTRACTOR'S
APPLICATION

50.1
The *C*'s application for
payment is for the
amount due since the
last payment

B
Sheet 1

Is it the first
application for
payment?

YES

The first application for
payment is for the
amount due

NO

Other applications are
for the change in the
amount due since the
previous payment

50.3
The *E* corrects any wrongly
assessed amount due

CORRECTIONS TO
WRONGLY ASSESSED
AMOUNTS

Is
there a wrongly
assessed amount
due?

YES

NO

50.3
The *E* notifies the *C*
of the correction
before paying the *C*

FC 13
Communications

FC 51
Payment

Finish

Flow chart 50 Sheet 2 of 2
Assessing the amount due

Flow chart 51
Payment

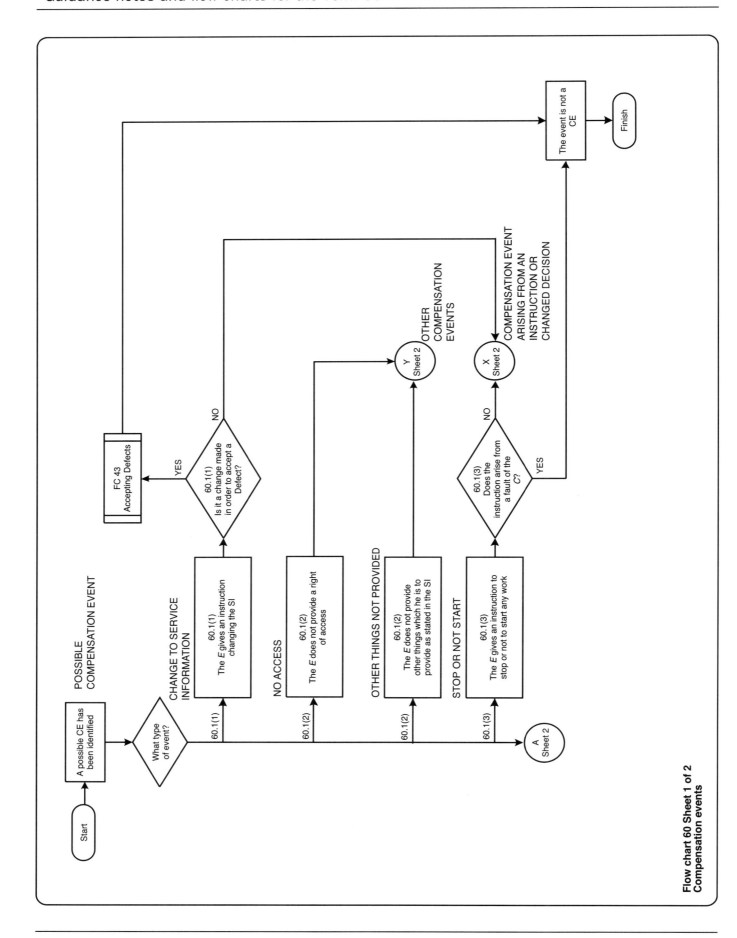

Flow chart 60 Sheet 1 of 2
Compensation events

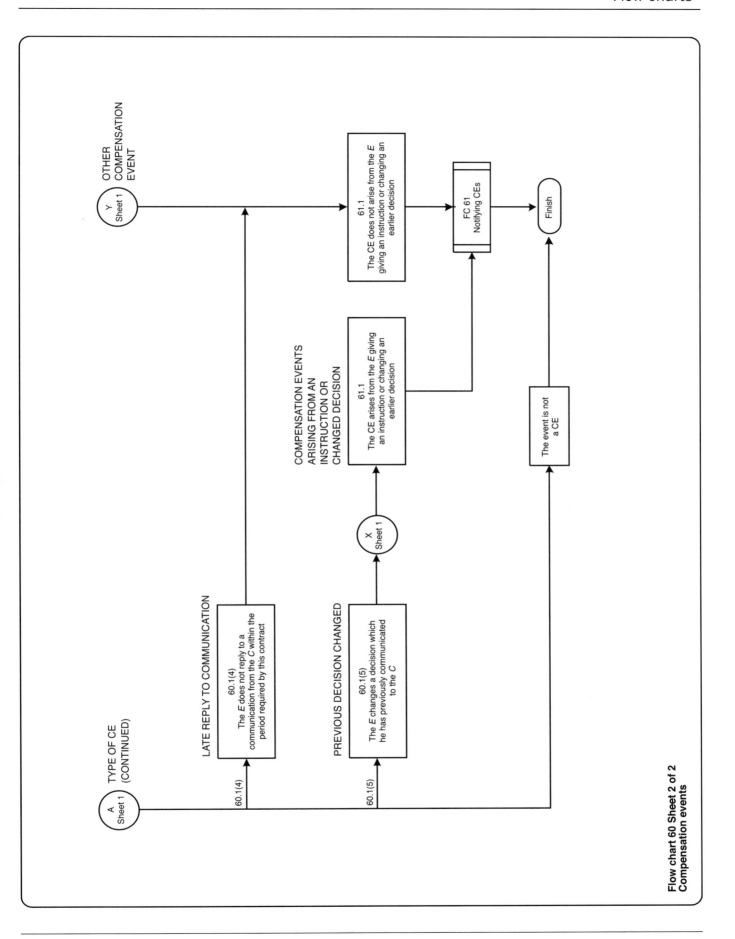

Flow chart 60 Sheet 2 of 2
Compensation events

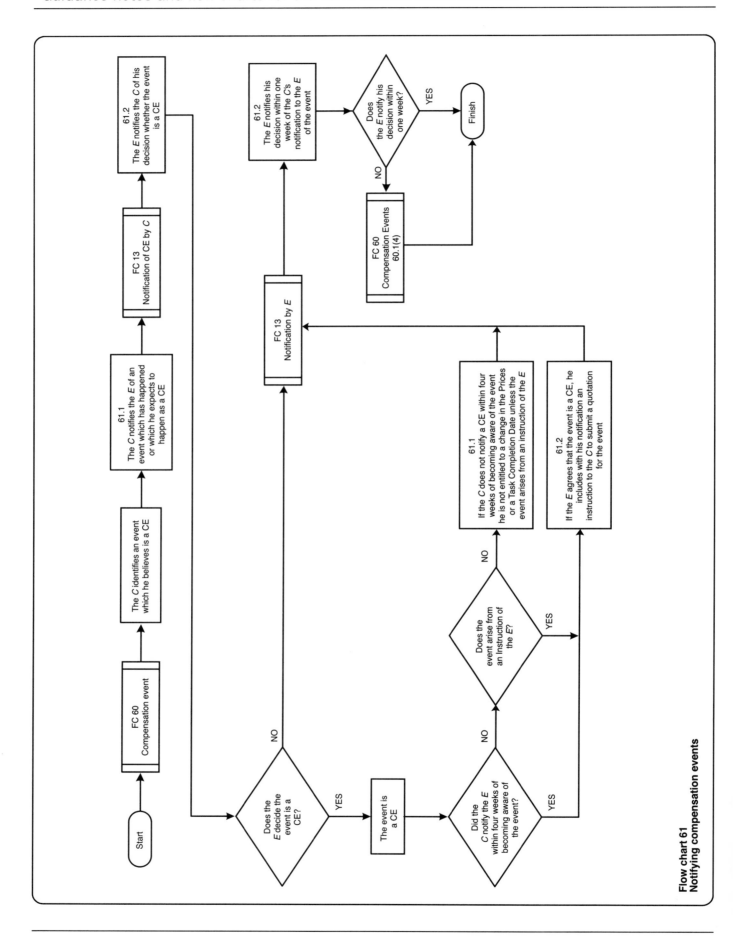

Flow chart 61
Notifying compensation events

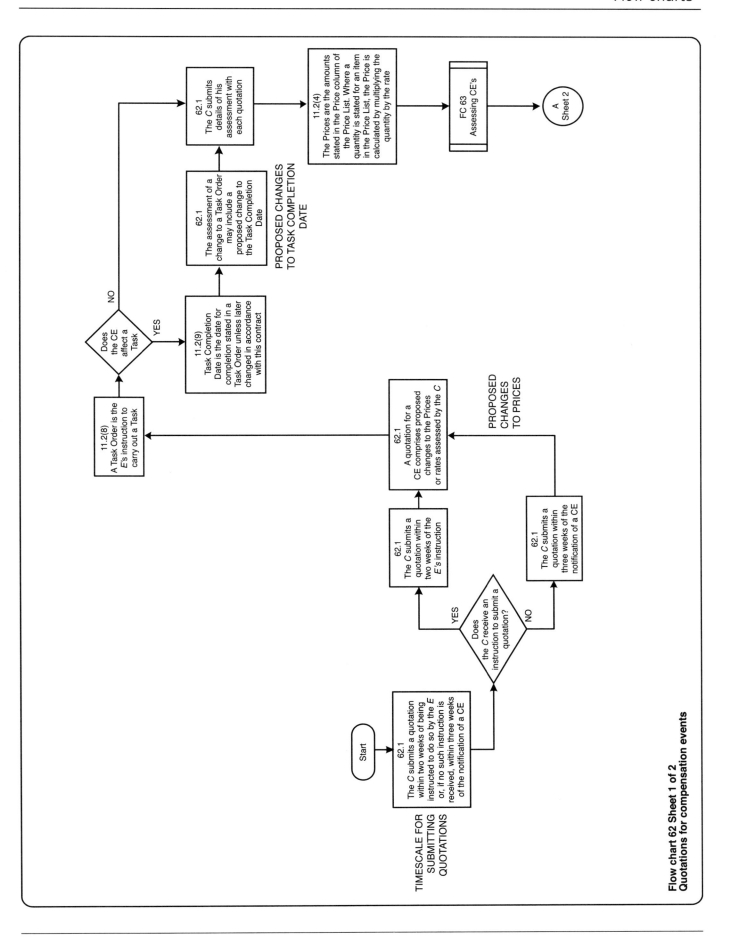

Flow chart 62 Sheet 1 of 2
Quotations for compensation events

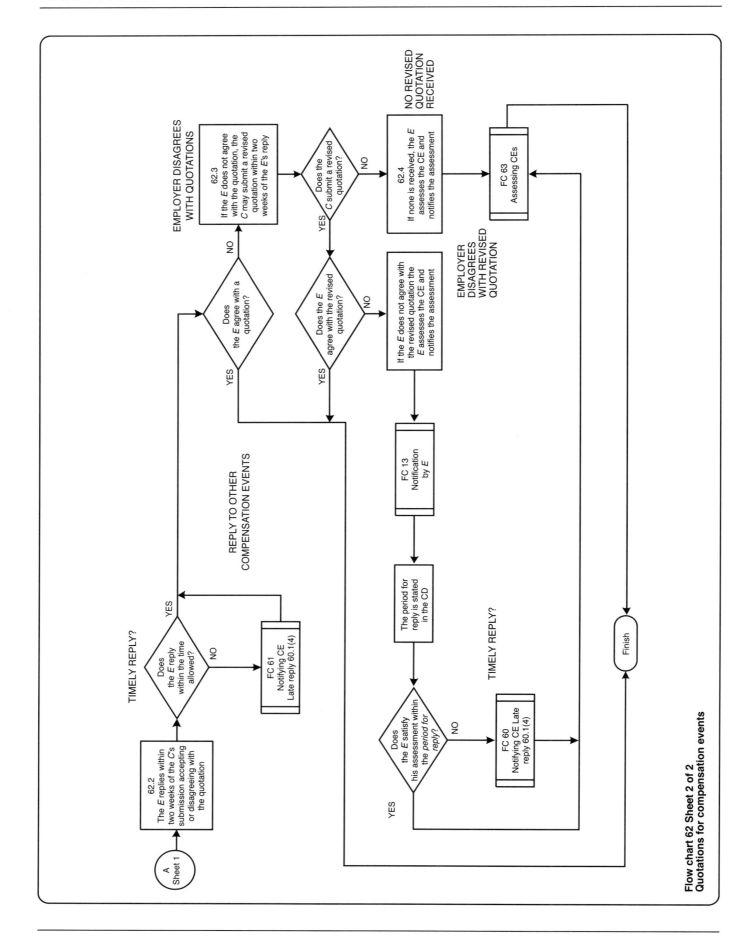

Flow chart 62 Sheet 2 of 2
Quotations for compensation events

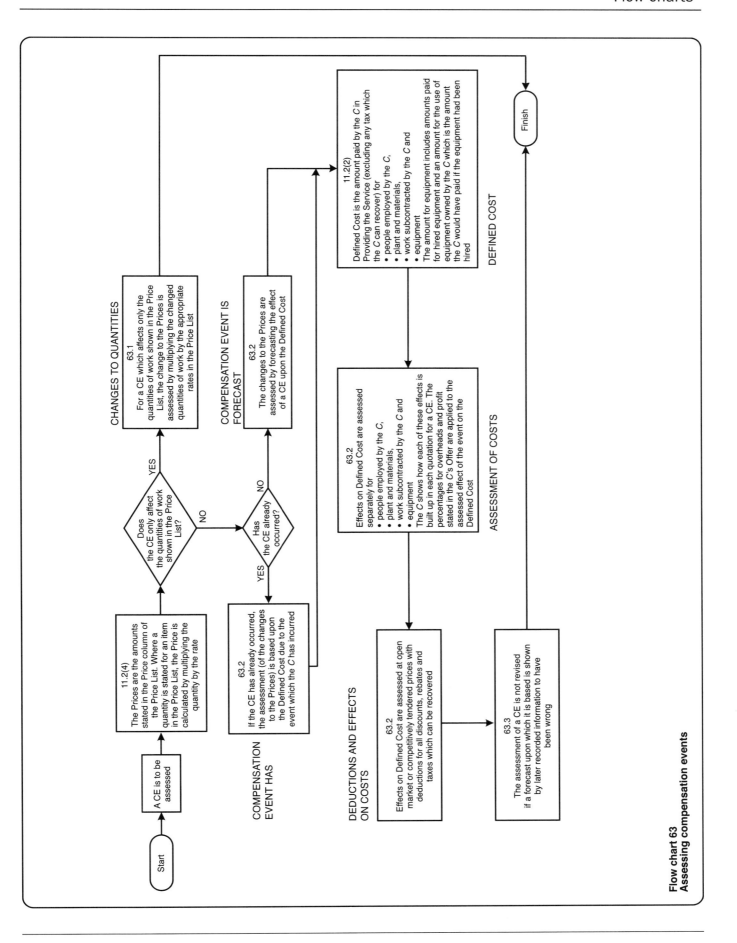

Flow chart 63
Assessing compensation events

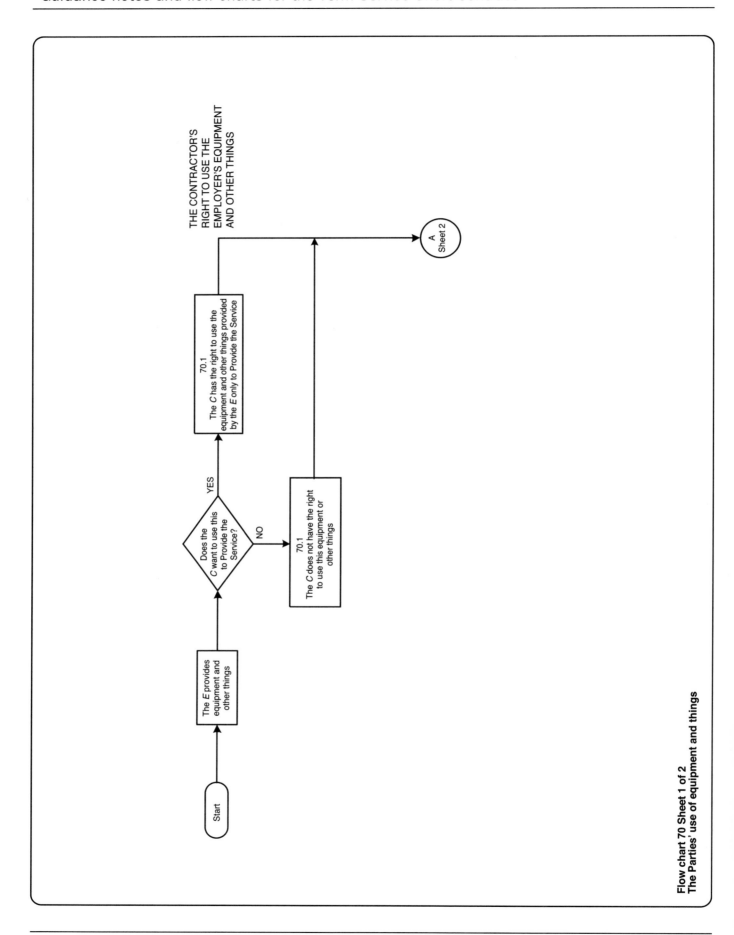

THE CONTRACTOR'S
RIGHT TO USE THE
EMPLOYER'S EQUIPMENT
AND OTHER THINGS

Start

The *E* provides
equipment and
other things

Does the
C want to use this
to Provide the
Service?

YES

NO

70.1
The *C* has the right to use the
equipment and other things provided
by the *E* only to Provide the Service

70.1
The *C* does not have the right
to use this equipment or
other things

A
Sheet 2

Flow chart 70 Sheet 1 of 2
The Parties' use of equipment and things

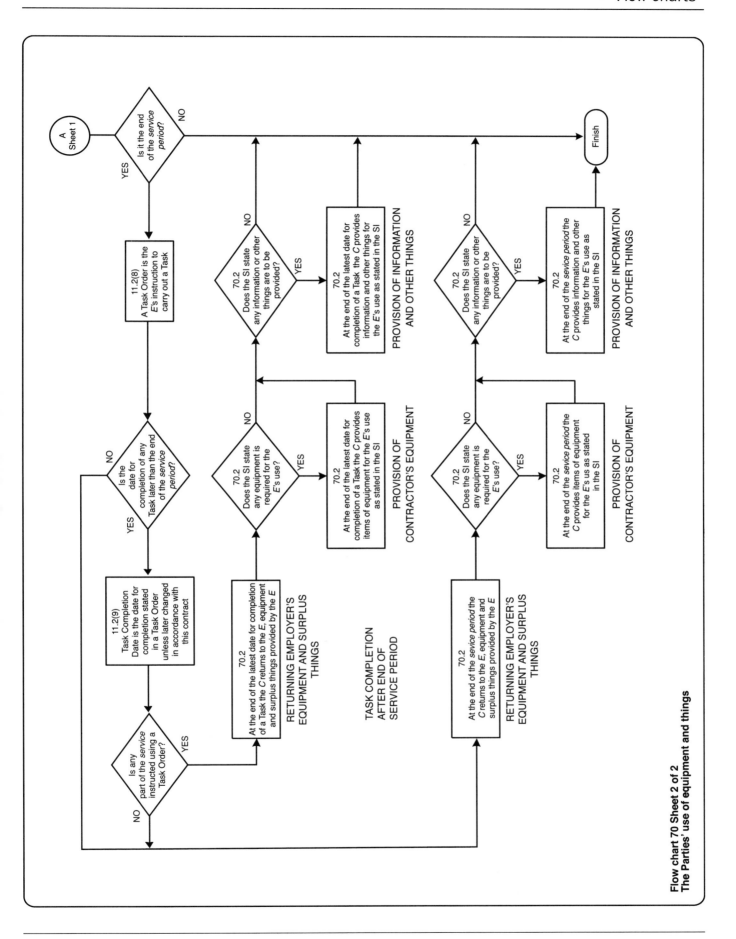

Flow chart 70 Sheet 2 of 2
The Parties' use of equipment and things

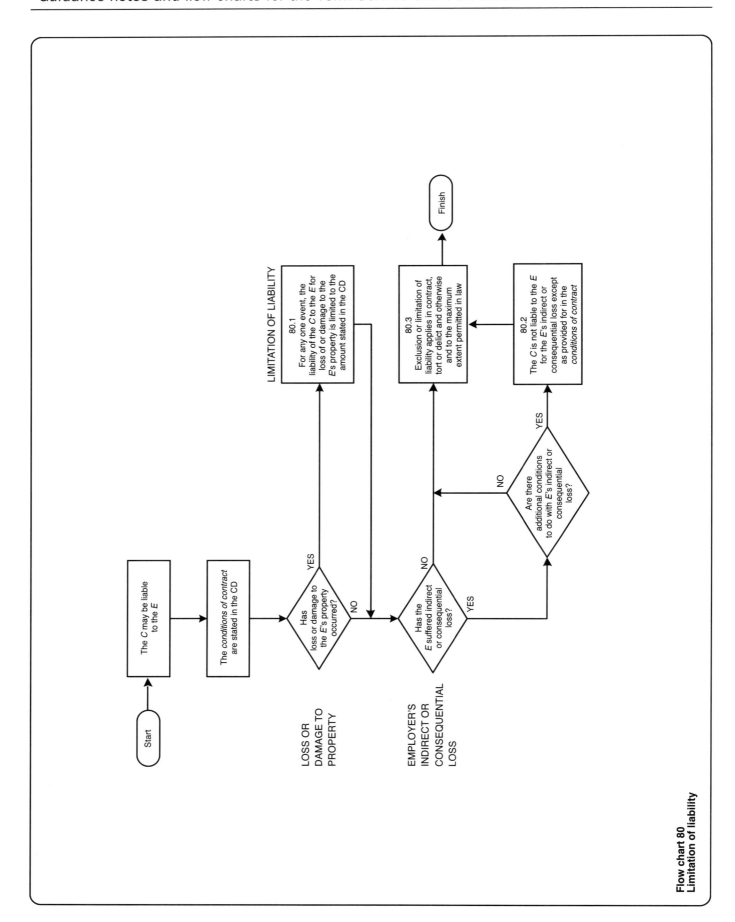

LIMITATION OF LIABILITY

Start

The *C* may be liable to the *E*

The *conditions of contract* are stated in the CD

LOSS OR DAMAGE TO PROPERTY

Has loss or damage to the *E*'s property occurred?

YES → 80.1 For any one event, the liability of the *C* to the *E* for loss of or damage to the *E*'s property is limited to the amount stated in the CD

NO

EMPLOYER'S INDIRECT OR CONSEQUENTIAL LOSS

Has the *E* suffered indirect or consequential loss?

NO

YES → Are there additional conditions to do with *E*'s indirect or consequential loss?

NO → 80.3 Exclusion or limitation of liability applies in contract, tort or delict and otherwise and to the maximum extent permitted in law → Finish

YES → 80.2 The *C* is not liable to the *E* for the *E*'s indirect or consequential loss except as provided for in the *conditions of contract*

Flow chart 80
Limitation of liability

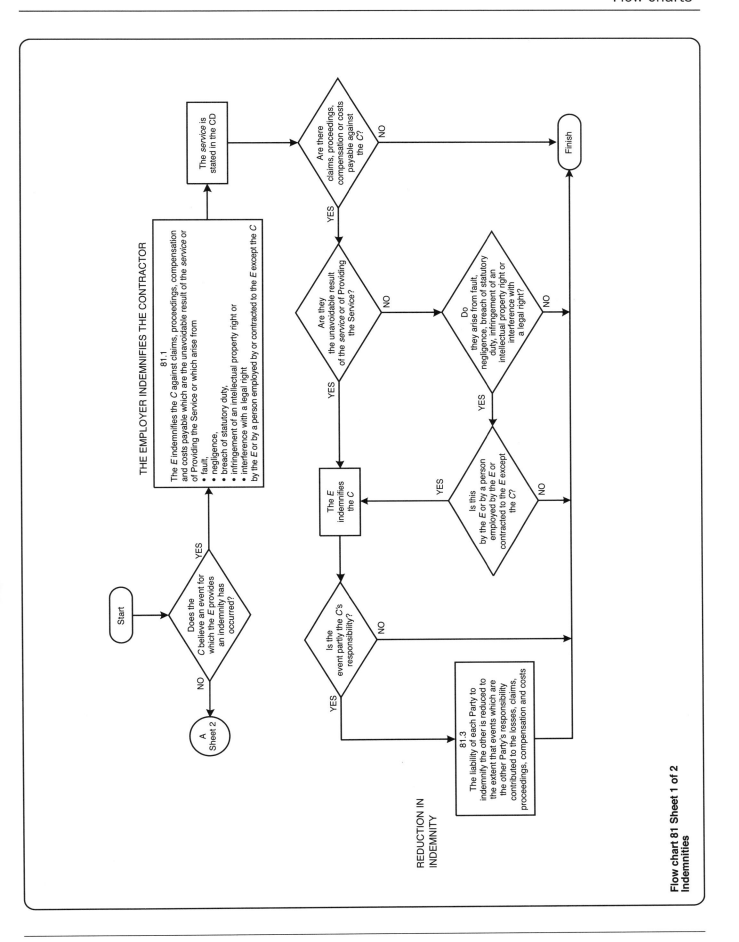

THE EMPLOYER INDEMNIFIES THE CONTRACTOR

Start

Does the *C* believe an event for which the *E* provides an indemnity has occurred?

NO → A Sheet 2

YES →

81.1

The *E* indemnifies the *C* against claims, proceedings, compensation and costs payable which are the unavoidable result of the *service* or of Providing the Service or which arise from
- fault,
- negligence,
- breach of statutory duty,
- infringement of an intellectual property right or
- interference with a legal right

by the *E* or by a person employed by or contracted to the *E* except the *C*

The *service* is stated in the CD

Are there claims, proceedings, compensation or costs payable against the *C*?

NO → Finish

YES →

Are they the unavoidable result of the *service* or of Providing the Service?

YES → The *E* indemnifies the *C*

NO →

Do they arise from fault, negligence, breach of statutory duty, infringement of an intellectual property right or interference with a legal right?

NO → Finish

YES →

Is this by the *E* or by a person employed by the *E* or contracted to the *E* except the *C*?

YES → The *E* indemnifies the *C*

NO → Finish

Is the event partly the *C*'s responsibility?

YES →

NO →

REDUCTION IN INDEMNITY

81.3

The liability of each Party to indemnify the other is reduced to the extent that events which are the other Party's responsibility contributed to the losses, claims, proceedings, compensation and costs

Flow chart 81 Sheet 1 of 2
Indemnities

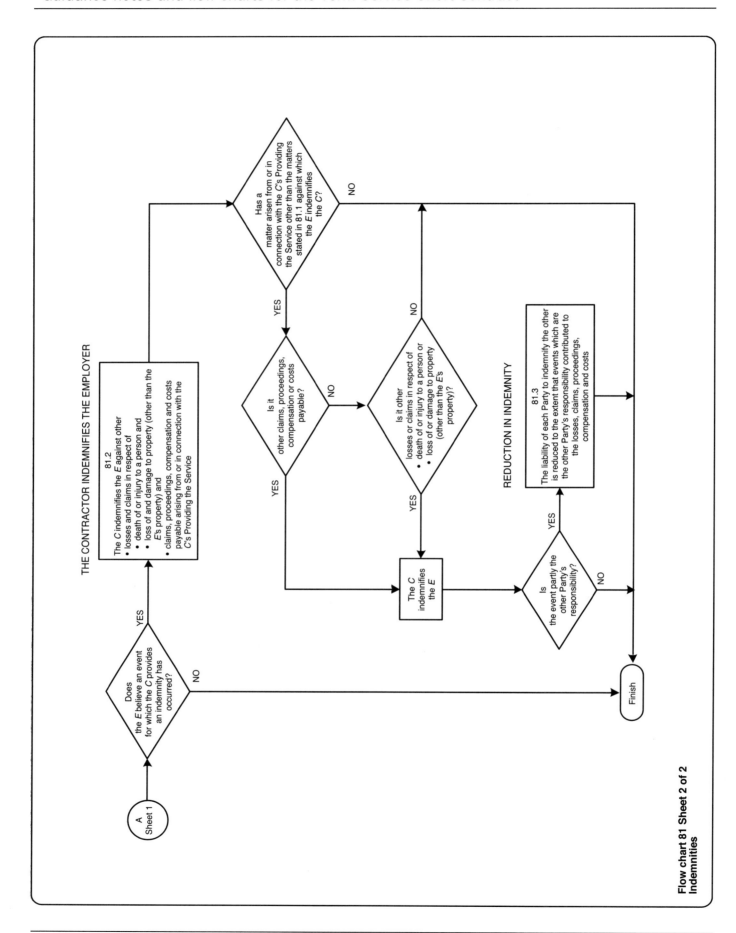

**Flow chart 81 Sheet 2 of 2
Indemnities**

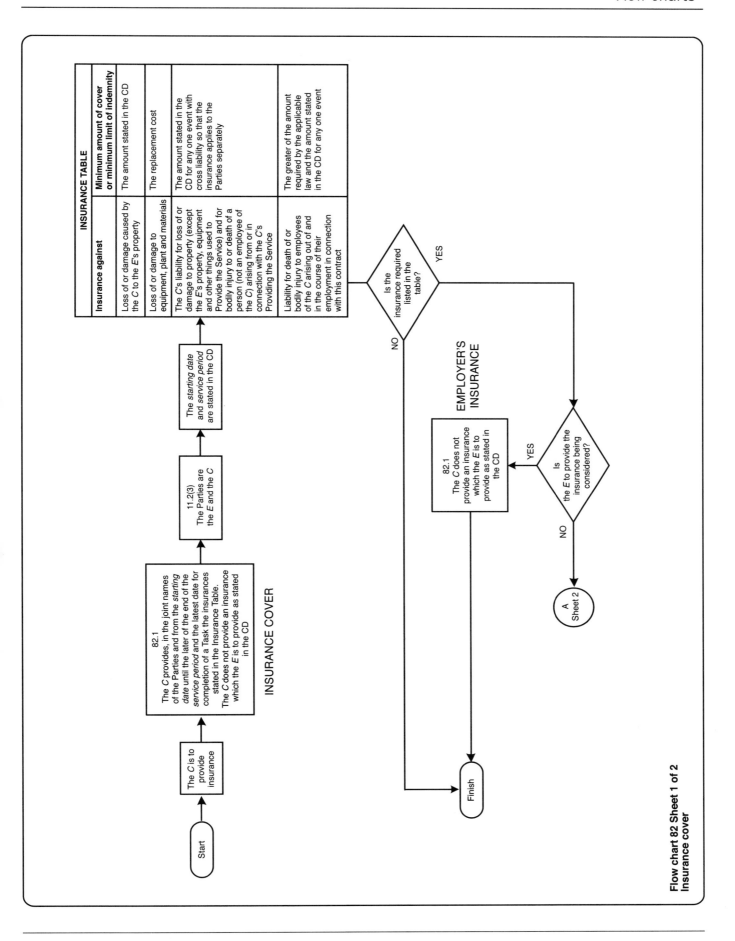

INSURANCE TABLE

Insurance against	Minimum amount of cover or minimum limit of indemnity
Loss of or damage caused by the C to the E's property	The amount stated in the CD
Loss of or damage to equipment, plant and materials	The replacement cost
The C's liability for loss of or damage to property (except the E's property, equipment and other things used to Provide the Service) and for bodily injury to or death of a person (not an employee of the C) arising from or in connection with the C's Providing the Service	The amount stated in the CD for any one event with cross liability so that the insurance applies to the Parties separately
Liability for death of or bodily injury to employees of the C arising out of and in the course of their employment in connection with this contract	The greater of the amount required by the applicable law and the amount stated in the CD for any one event

INSURANCE COVER

Start

The C is to provide insurance

82.1
The C provides, in the joint names of the Parties and from the *starting date* until the later of the end of the *service period* and the latest date for completion of a Task the insurances stated in the Insurance Table.
The C does not provide an insurance which the E is to provide as stated in the CD

11.2(3)
The Parties are the E and the C

The *starting date* and *service period* are stated in the CD

Is the insurance required listed in the table?

NO → Finish

YES

EMPLOYER'S INSURANCE

Is the E to provide the insurance being considered?

YES →
82.1
The C does not provide an insurance which the E is to provide as stated in the CD
→ Finish

NO →
A
Sheet 2

**Flow chart 82 Sheet 1 of 2
Insurance cover**

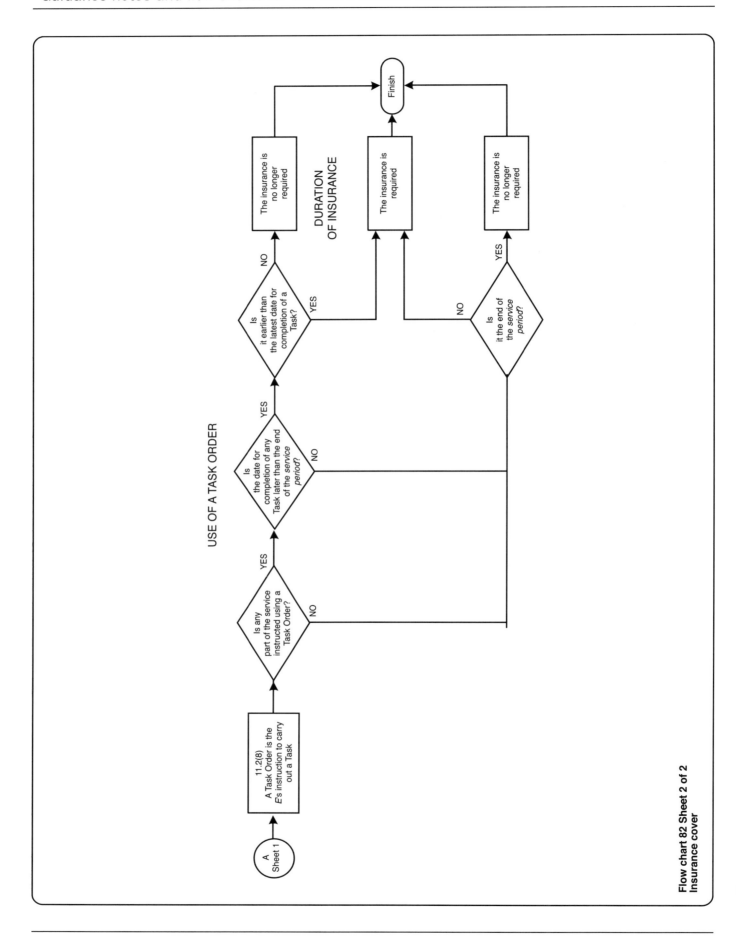

USE OF A TASK ORDER

DURATION OF INSURANCE

11.2(8)
A Task Order is the
E's instruction to carry
out a Task

A
Sheet 1

Is any
part of the service
instructed using a
Task Order?

Is
the date for
completion of any
Task later than the end
of the *service
period*?

Is
it earlier than
the latest date for
completion of a
Task?

Is
it the end of
the *service
period*?

The insurance is
no longer
required

The insurance is
required

The insurance is
no longer
required

Finish

Flow chart 82 Sheet 2 of 2
Insurance cover

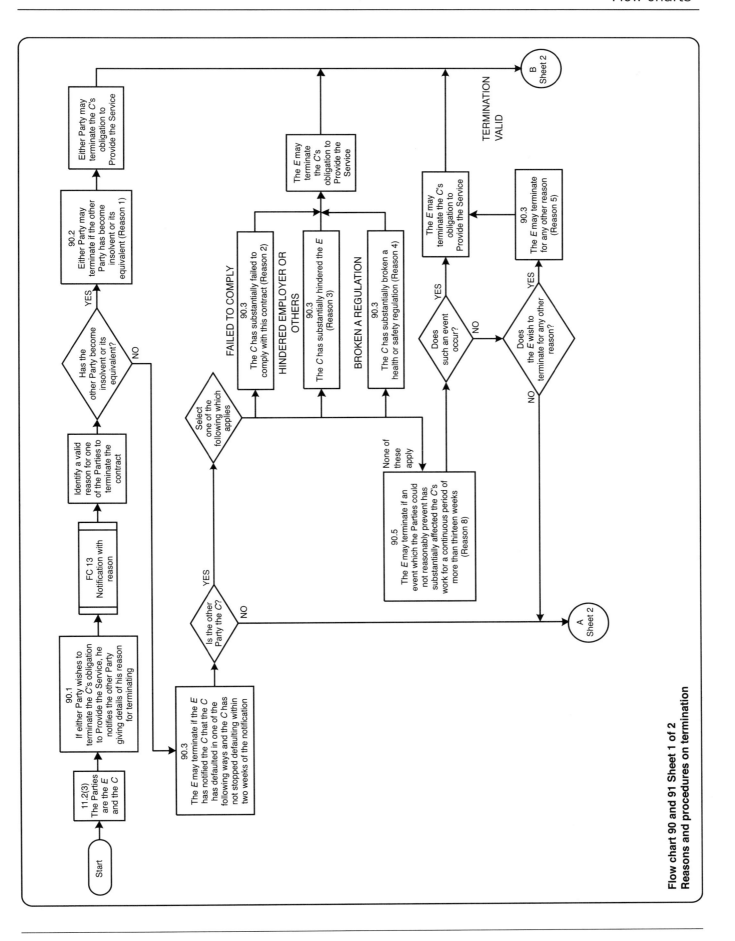

Flow chart 90 and 91 Sheet 1 of 2
Reasons and procedures on termination

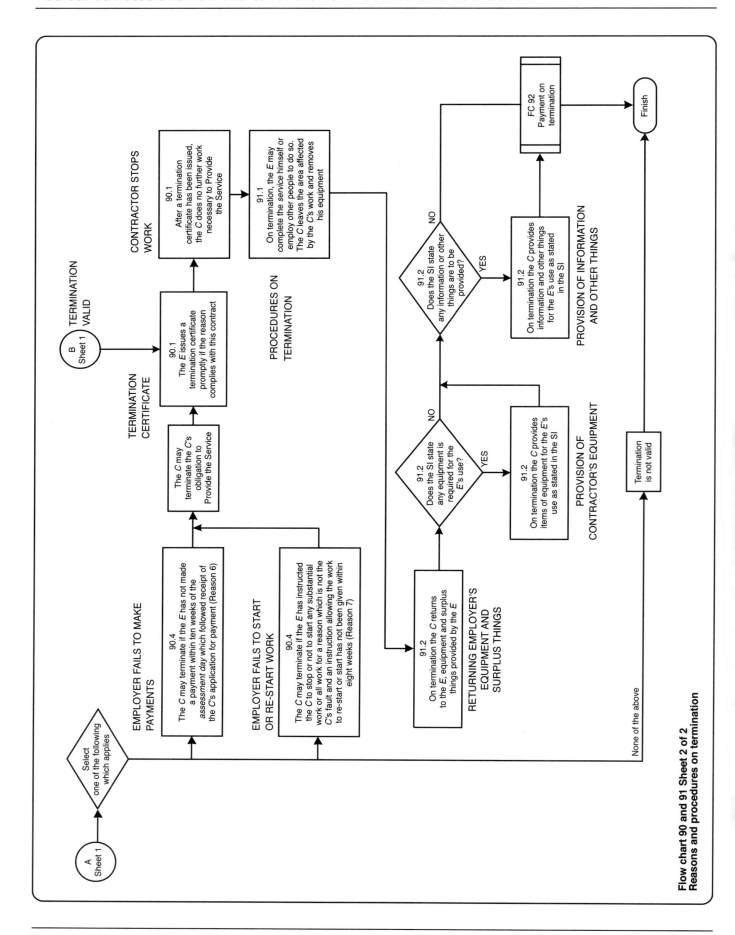

B
Sheet 1

TERMINATION
VALID

A
Sheet 1

Select one of the following which applies

TERMINATION
CERTIFICATE

CONTRACTOR STOPS
WORK

EMPLOYER FAILS TO MAKE
PAYMENTS

90.4
The *C* may terminate if the *E* has not made a payment within ten weeks of the *assessment day* which followed receipt of the *C*'s application for payment (Reason 6)

EMPLOYER FAILS TO START
OR RE-START WORK

90.4
The *C* may terminate if the *E* has instructed the *C* to stop or not to start any substantial work or all work for a reason which is not the *C*'s fault and an instruction allowing the work to re-start or start has not been given within eight weeks (Reason 7)

The *C* may terminate the *C*'s obligation to Provide the Service

90.1
The *E* issues a termination certificate promptly if the reason complies with this contract

90.1
After a termination certificate has been issued, the *C* does no further work necessary to Provide the Service

91.1
On termination, the *E* may complete the *service* himself or employ other people to do so. The *C* leaves the area affected by the *C*'s work and removes his equipment

PROCEDURES ON
TERMINATION

91.2
On termination the *C* returns to the *E*, equipment and surplus things provided by the *E*

RETURNING EMPLOYER'S
EQUIPMENT AND
SURPLUS THINGS

91.2
Does the SI state any equipment is required for the *E*'s use? — NO

YES

91.2
On termination the *C* provides items of equipment for the *E*'s use as stated in the SI

PROVISION OF
CONTRACTOR'S EQUIPMENT

91.2
Does the SI state any information or other things are to be provided? — NO

YES

91.2
On termination the *C* provides information and other things for the *E*'s use as stated in the SI

PROVISION OF INFORMATION
AND OTHER THINGS

FC 92
Payment on
termination

Finish

Termination
is not valid

None of the above

Flow chart 90 and 91 Sheet 2 of 2
Reasons and procedures on termination

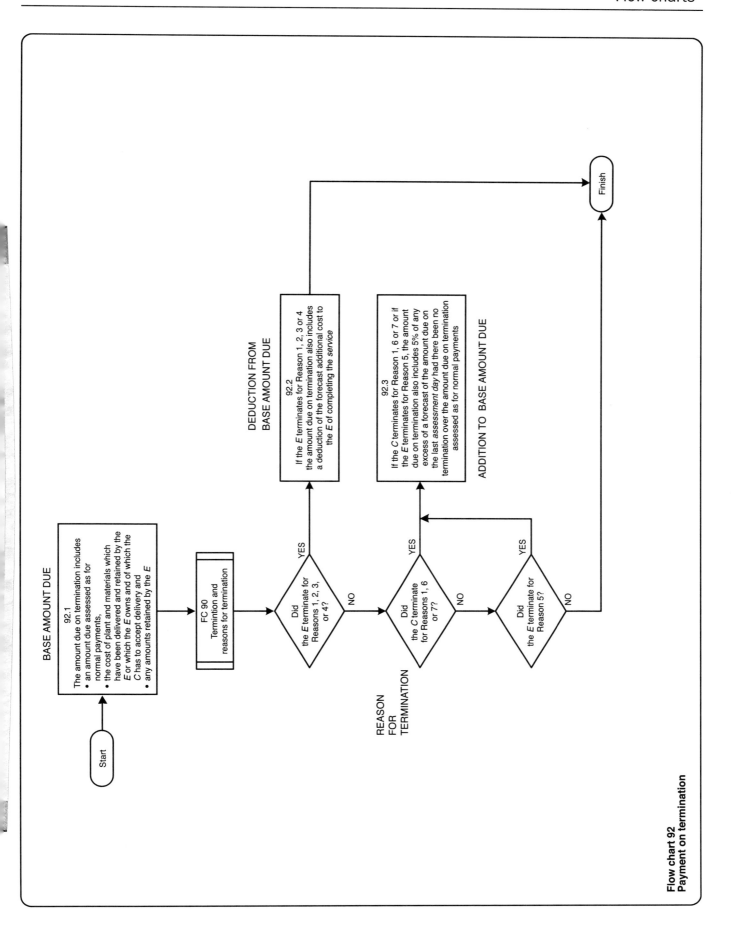

Start

BASE AMOUNT DUE

92.1
The amount due on termination includes
• an amount due assessed as for normal payments,
• the cost of plant and materials which have been delivered and retained by the *E* or which the *E* owns and of which the *C* has to accept delivery and
• any amounts retained by the *E*

FC 90
Termination and reasons for termination

Did the *E* terminate for Reasons 1, 2, 3, or 4?

REASON FOR TERMINATION

Did the *C* terminate for Reasons 1, 6 or 7?

Did the *E* terminate for Reason 5?

YES

NO

YES

NO

YES

NO

DEDUCTION FROM BASE AMOUNT DUE

92.2
If the *E* terminates for Reason 1, 2, 3 or 4 the amount due on termination also includes a deduction of the forecast additional cost to the *E* of completing the *service*

92.3
If the *C* terminates for Reason 1, 6 or 7 or if the *E* terminates for Reason 5, the amount due on termination also includes 5% of any excess of a forecast of the amount due on the last *assessment day* had there been no termination over the amount due on termination assessed as for normal payments

ADDITION TO BASE AMOUNT DUE

Finish

Flow chart 92
Payment on termination

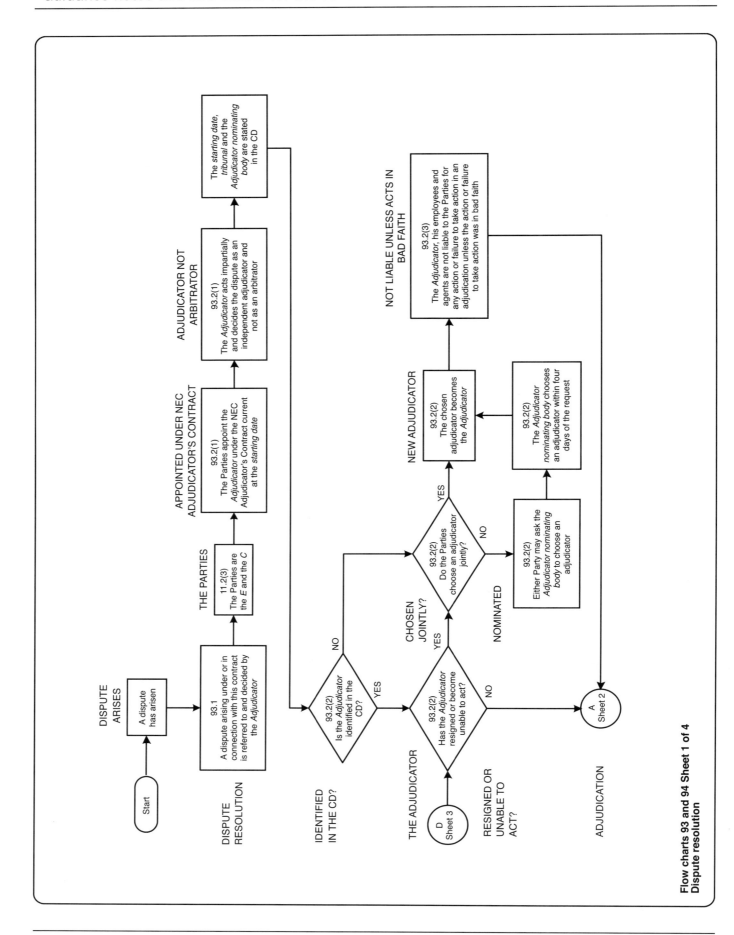

DISPUTE ARISES

Start

A dispute has arisen

DISPUTE RESOLUTION

93.1
A dispute arising under or in connection with this contract is referred to and decided by the *Adjudicator*

THE PARTIES

11.2(3)
The Parties are the *E* and the *C*

APPOINTED UNDER NEC ADJUDICATOR'S CONTRACT

93.2(1)
The Parties appoint the *Adjudicator* under the NEC Adjudicator's Contract current at the *starting date*

ADJUDICATOR NOT ARBITRATOR

93.2(1)
The *Adjudicator* acts impartially and decides the dispute as an independent adjudicator and not as an arbitrator

The *starting date*, *tribunal* and the *Adjudicator nominating body* are stated in the CD

IDENTIFIED IN THE CD?

93.2(2)
Is the *Adjudicator* identified in the CD?

YES / NO

THE ADJUDICATOR

93.2(2)
Has the *Adjudicator* resigned or become unable to act?

RESIGNED OR UNABLE TO ACT?

D
Sheet 3

CHOSEN JOINTLY?

93.2(2)
Do the Parties choose an adjudicator jointly?

YES / NO

NOMINATED

93.2(2)
Either Party may ask the *Adjudicator nominating body* to choose an adjudicator

93.2(2)
The *Adjudicator nominating body* chooses an adjudicator within four days of the request

NEW ADJUDICATOR

93.2(2)
The chosen adjudicator becomes the *Adjudicator*

NOT LIABLE UNLESS ACTS IN BAD FAITH

93.2(3)
The *Adjudicator*, his employees and agents are not liable to the Parties for any action or failure to take action in an adjudication unless the action or failure to take action was in bad faith

ADJUDICATION

A
Sheet 2

Flow charts 93 and 94 Sheet 1 of 4
Dispute resolution

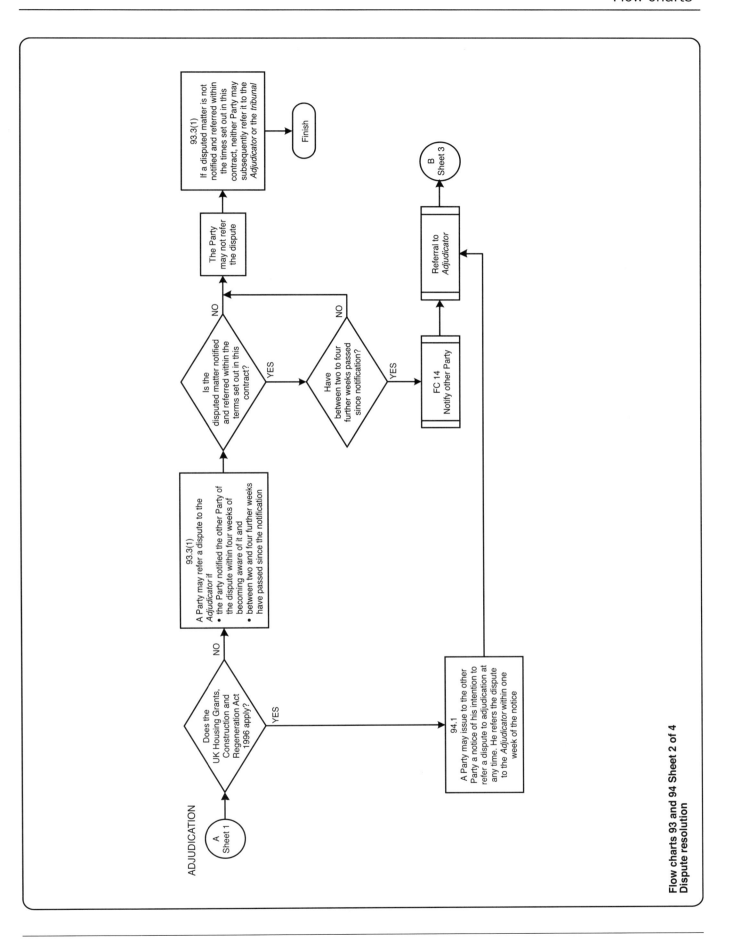

ADJUDICATION

A
Sheet 1

Does the
UK Housing Grants,
Construction and
Regeneration Act
1996 apply?

NO

YES

93.3(1)
A Party may refer a dispute to the
Adjudicator if
• the Party notified the other Party of
the dispute within four weeks of
becoming aware of it and
• between two and four further weeks
have passed since the notification

Is the
disputed matter notified
and referred within the
terms set out in this
contract?

NO

YES

The Party
may not refer
the dispute

93.3(1)
If a disputed matter is not
notified and referred within
the times set out in this
contract, neither Party may
subsequently refer it to the
Adjudicator or the *tribunal*

Finish

Have
between two to four
further weeks passed
since notification?

NO

YES

FC 14
Notify other Party

Referral to
Adjudicator

B
Sheet 3

94.1
A Party may issue to the other
Party a notice of his intention to
refer a dispute to adjudication at
any time. He refers the dispute
to the *Adjudicator* within one
week of the notice

Flow charts 93 and 94 Sheet 2 of 4
Dispute resolution

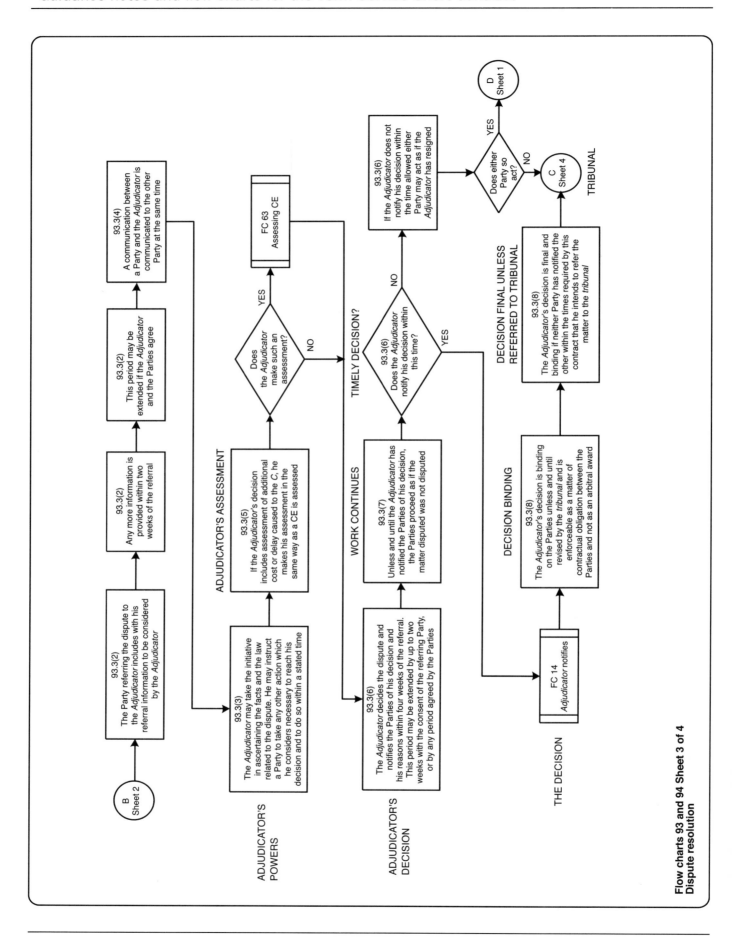

Flow charts 93 and 94 Sheet 3 of 4
Dispute resolution

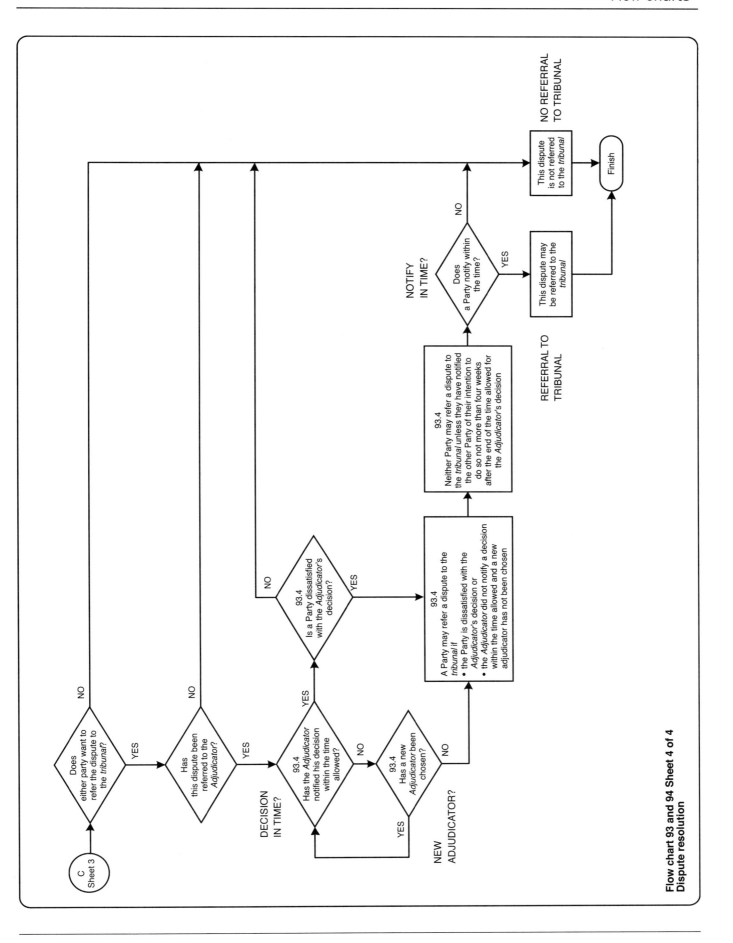

Flow chart 93 and 94 Sheet 4 of 4
Dispute resolution